nemouth

The Job Interview Toolkit

Careertrain Publishing

By the same Authors:

The One to One Toolkit: Tips and Strategies for Advisers,
Coaches and Mentors
Julie Cooper and Ann Reynolds ISBN 978
If your job involved helping people move forward in their lives or
career, this book is for you. It takes you step by step through a tried
and trusted model for giving advice, then provides a more in depth
model for digging deeper. Part Three is the Toolkit, a collection of
bite size ideas, tips and strategies for dealing with different types of
clients.

**The Groupwork Toolkit: How to convert your one to one
advice skills to work with groups**
Ann Reynolds and Julie Cooper ISBN 978 0955968013
This book is essential for coaches and advisers who may have to
work with more than one client at a time. It de-mystifies groupwork,
showing you how to plan and run a successful session.

By Julie Cooper:

**Face to Face in the Workplace: A Handbook of Strategies for
Effective Discussions**
Julie Cooper ISBN 978 0955968037
This highly acclaimed book has won praise from many sources and
is rapidly becoming adopted as a key reference tool, both for busy
managers and also students on business courses.

**Five Steps to being Heard: How to get your message across
to the right person**
Julie Cooper ISBN 978 0955968099
Do you sometimes get taken for granted or overlooked? Are you
always recognised for the talents you bring? If you want someone to
hear your message, then this is the book for you. It will help you
identify why your message isn't always being heard, and give you
strategies to makes sure the people who matter hear what you have
to say.

All titles are available at www.springpublishing.co.uk

The Job Interview Toolkit

Toolkit

Exercises
to get you fit for your interview

Ann Reynolds and Julie Cooper

© Copyright Ann Reynolds and Julie Cooper 2012

Illustrations by Becky Gilbey

ISBN 978-0-9559680-2-0

Published by Careertrain Publishing
www.springpublishing.co.uk
info@careertrain.net

Note: The material contained in this book is set out in good faith for general guidance only and no liability can be accepted for loss or expense incurred as a result of relying in particular circumstances on statements made in this book.

Printed and bound in England

Contents

Who are Ann and Julie?

We are career coaches, advisers and trainers who first worked together in the Cambridgeshire Adult Guidance Service. Later we each established our own consultancies, providing advice and training to people in many different situations – redundancy, unemployment or in their workplace. We came together again in 2007 to offer training and qualifications in Advice and Guidance, which led to writing two books: "The One to One Toolkit" and "The Groupwork Toolkit", both for advisers.

Julie came from a training background and Ann started as a careers adviser offering one-to-one support. We have both designed and run Job Interview training days as well as coaching people who have been invited to interview and are worried about their performance. Our format has helped people at many different career levels. We can include customer service advisers, warehouse staff, social workers, accountants and senior managers among them. What they learn with us has boosted their confidence and shown them how to prepare. They report that their performance was far better than before and often that they get the job.

Our format is based on a simple system we now call **TAPAS**. We want to share this with you, so that in your interview you will be the best you can be, let the real you shine out, impress the interviewers and get that job.

Thanks

Of the many people who have helped us along the way, we may not have been writing this book without the help of two in particular. Sue Claydon has been a leader in the Cambridgeshire adult guidance through many changes and not only gave both of us a job but encouraged us to develop our skills and new ways of working. Belinda Coaten, trainer, career coach and image consultant, joined forces with Ann over many years to work with people facing redundancy, introducing her to STAR Stories and the importance of image, as well as excellence in training skills. Thank you to both.

Finally, we would like to dedicate this book to our own young people who are working hard establishing their careers: Katy, Bryony, Thomas and Vanessa. Good luck and may you continue to navigate your career paths creatively and successfully, getting as much fun from them as we have from ours.

Foreword

Congratulations, you have been invited for interview!

You must have written a good application form or sent a well worded letter or email with a clear, concise CV. Maybe you have avoided doing too much work so far – perhaps an agency or a colleague has put you forward for a job they think you will do well. Whichever it is, the employer likes the sound of you and they want to meet you in person. So, you now have to face the next challenge.

Does anyone like job interviews? Most people hate them! Our natural response is to bury our heads in the sand – every time we remember the dreaded date is getting closer, we find something else to do, to take our minds off it. Then afterwards, it is all...

- I didn't expect that question
- I wish I'd told them about...
- I just rambled on, I think they were bored
- They completely threw me
- I didn't do myself justice
- I felt so nervous
- I dried up, I couldn't think of anything to say
- If only I'd thought about...
- If only I'd prepared

If you have picked up this book, it is because you are looking for a better way. That way is – **preparation**.

This Toolkit has been designed to help you prepare your interview performance. It aims to give you the best possible chance of getting the job you really want.

Do we really need another book about job interviews?

An online search will reveal thousands of books and videos giving advice and hints about interviews. Many of these are excellent (there is a list of some of our favourites at the back) and with so many already out there, how is this one different?

The Job Interview Toolkit is not...
• an in-depth explanation of every different type of interview
• a list of interview questions and perfect answers
• a long list of do's and don'ts
• something to read from cover to cover

So what is it? We call it a Toolkit because it is just that, a set of tools to help you prepare for your next job interview. The tools are practical things to do, which have been used by people at "Do Better in Job Interview" courses and in one-to-one coaching. Some of the tools are paper and pencil exercises. If you write down your ideas, either in the book or on a sheet of paper, they are more likely to stick in your mind for when you will need them – at the interview!

The Job Interview Toolkit is based on two simple facts:
1. **The employer needs** something - someone to do a job for them
2. **The employer can choose** - the person they believe will do the job better than anyone else.

Where do you fit in? You want the job. Since the employer can choose, you will have to make sure they choose you. How? You cannot make them, so you will have to **persuade** them.

As any good salesperson will tell you, before you can persuade someone, you first have to **understand** them and **their needs**.

The Job Interview Toolkit offers you **TAPAS**, a five-step system to help you **UP** your game by:
1. **Understanding** what the employer needs
2. **Persuading** the employer that YOU can meet their needs.

The 5-Step TAPAS System

Think Analyse Prepare Adjust   Shine

1. **Think** like an Employer

We know that if you want to persuade someone, you first have to understand them and know what they need. To understand them, you need to step into their shoes, look through their eyes and see how it feels to be them. Our first set of tools will help you step into the employer's shoes and see the world from their point of view.

2. **Analyse** the Job

Knowing what the customer needs is the second tool in the salesperson's toolkit. If I am selling you a pair of trousers and I know it is really important to you to appear your best when you go out this Saturday, I will tell you how good you look in them. I will not bother to tell you how well made they are, or how long they will last – both may be true, but not what you need at this moment. This section gives you the tools to analyse the job so you understand what the employer needs most at this time.

3. **Prepare** your Evidence

The employer will not believe you are wonderful just because you say so. You will have to give them evidence to back up your claims to be brilliant at what they need you to do. This section gives you some tools to help gather relevant evidence, then it shows you how to present your evidence as a STAR story – describing it in a way that will totally convince and impress the employer.

4. **Adjust** to fit

After carefully analysing the job and collecting your evidence, you will, on paper, be ready to persuade the employer that you are the best person for this job. Looking good on paper is a start – it is what got you through to interview. Now you have to look good in real life.

Research into communication has shown that people are more convinced by what they **see** and **feel** than by the words they hear. Here we show you how to adjust your image so that you look the part and adjust your mindset so that you feel confident in the part. It is not easy to feel positive and passionate about what you are saying when you are tense and nervous under the interview spotlight. To help you, there is a choice of tools that have been shown to help people put across their real personality and passion in the interview.

5. **Shine** like a STAR

If you have used some of the tools in the first four parts of this book, you have a very good chance of putting in a star performance and showing yourself at your best. In this section you will learn how to observe other people's behaviour and carefully manage your own, to make sure you shine most strongly when it will have the greatest impact. You can follow the timeline of an interview to see what happens when, and work out how to insert your **STAR** stories at just the right moment.

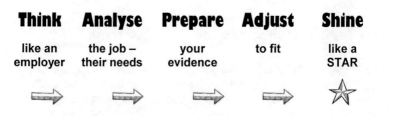

Think	**Analyse**	**Prepare**	**Adjust**	**Shine**
like an employer	the job – their needs	your evidence	to fit	like a STAR

We will look at each of these steps in turn and give you some tools for each, but first we will think about you.

Interviews – What are you afraid of?

Highlight any that are true for you, and add your own.

Different people have different fears

What did you answer? Who are you more like...

Chatty Charlie? or **Careful Cara?**

Careful Cara

If you are most worried about getting it wrong, being tongue-tied or feeling shy, you may be more like Cara. Well-organised, thoughtful and hardworking, Cara is a dream employee. She gets things done, she does them well, and she meets targets for both numbers and quality. She usually writes a really good application and often gets short-listed for interview.

The interview is where it can go wrong for Cara. Her strong commitment to doing things well can make her anxious in this unfamiliar situation where she will have to think on her feet. Perhaps she is modest and feels uncomfortable showing off about how good she is. She feels tense and this has the effect of freezing her. She says very little and appears stiff and unfriendly.

At times like this, she wishes she could be more like...

Chatty Charlie

Lively and fun, Charlie shines in social situations. He has an excellent way with words and people quickly warm to him. This gives him an edge over Cara in the first moments of the interview. It so happens that the first moments of any meeting are those people remember most vividly, so this is good news for Charlie.

It gets more difficult for him as the interview goes on and the employer wants to dig deeper to find out what he can actually do for them. Charlie may be so used to winning people round with his charm that there is no need to back up his case with hard evidence. What he may fear at interview is rambling off the point, not knowing what they want, or appearing too lightweight. He might think the interview had gone really well because they had such a good conversation, and be shocked to hear he had not been selected.

(There are times when interviewers have been so charmed by a very skilful Charlie that they forget to check out his ability to do the job. Lucky Charlie – but this usually ends in tears a few weeks or months down the line).

Charlie and Cara are two extremes and you may be a mixture – a bit of both. The five **TAPAS** steps to a good interview will help both, in slightly different ways.

Step 1 – Think like an Employer

 Cara

Putting yourself into the employer's shoes will make them seem less scary. You'll realise they are just people like you with their own hopes and fears.

 Charlie

Seeing the interview through the employer's eyes will help you focus on what they are really thinking, so you know what they want to hear and see.

Step 2 – Analyse the Job

 Cara

Perhaps you have already carefully analysed the job, but the structured method will help you stick to the key points and give a clear message to convince the employer of your skills.

 **Charlie**

You'll think about the employer's needs in a more structured way, so that you can gather the evidence to prove your case. Your analytical, bullet-point method will show you are organised and business-like.

Step 3 – Prepare the Evidence

 Cara

 Charlie

You'll see your confidence grow as you find examples of how you can meet all the employer's needs. You'll practise telling stories around each example to show you at your best.

By choosing the right example to meet each of the employer's needs, you'll build on the picture of you as an analytical and clear thinker, who has a wealth of relevant experience.

Step 4 – Adjust your Mindset

 Cara

 Charlie

This will boost your confidence. You'll learn to impress the employers' hearts as well as their minds – not just with what you say but how you say it – how to act the part because you believe you are right for it.

You'll think about the impression you want to make at *this* interview, rather than just going into automatic pilot. You will think about how much of yourself to show – the part of you that shows how well you fit this job.

Step 5 – Shine like a STAR

 Cara

 Charlie

Knowing that you understand clearly what the employer wants, and have got evidence to prove it, will drive away your fears and let the STAR in the real you shine out.

Having thought this through, got your evidence in order and focused on the impression you want to make, you will give a professional STAR performance!

So now you have seen how the **TAPAS** five step method can help you improve your interview performance, whatever your usual style, you can start on the first step and take a look inside the interviewer's head.

Step 1 Think like an Employer

Your one and only task in the interview is to convince the person opposite you that they want you for the job.

The first step to persuading someone is to understand them. So how do you get inside their head and see things from their point of view?

Here is the first Tool in our Toolkit

Imagine…

… that you are looking for someone to work for you.

If you have been a boss, you will find this easy. Think back to a time when you recruited staff. Note down your thoughts and feelings as you prepared for the interview. What were you hoping to find?

I wanted someone who…

I didn't want anyone who…

If you find it hard to imagine being the boss, choose one of these scenarios. **Imagine you are looking for...**

a hairdresser to do your hair at home

someone to fix your computer

someone to care for your child while you are at work

someone to do your garden

Four or five people have phoned and you have arranged for them to come round this evening at half hour intervals. What is going through your head as you wait for the first to arrive? Note them in the thought bubbles.

What did you write? Here are some things people have said about:

Looking for a hairdresser …

- I want them to make me look good
- I don't want them to ruin my hair
- I want someone who understands the kind of style I like
- I want them to give me new ideas
- I hope they're friendly
- I don't want them to force their ideas on me
- I need someone who doesn't mind the kids or the mess

If I've got computer problems …

- I hope they'll explain it in language I can understand
- I need someone who really knows about computers
- I don't want someone who makes me feel stupid
- I hope they don't break it
- I need someone I can call on when I want them
- I need them to be clear about their charges

The person who looks after my children...

- I hope they're kind, lively, fun
- I hope the kids will like them
- It must be someone responsible – my child has got to be safe
- I want them to have the same ideas as me about raising children
- I want to find the house clean and tidy when I come home

How many of these did you want? Look at your wants and fears, and it is very likely that they were all about wanting someone who:

1. **Can**   Skilled, good at their job, capable, knowledgeable

2. **Wants to** Keen, cares about the job and is reliable

3. **Fits in** Easy to get on with, understands your needs, makes you feel comfortable, has a similar style and outlook.

It has been said that what employers want comes down to three things:

1. **Can** you do the job?

2. **Will** you do the job?

3. Will you **fit in**?

Put your "employer" hat back on and imagine you are sitting at home waiting for your applicants to arrive – your hairdressers, IT people, childminders or gardeners. There is a ring at the door and you go to open it. What do you see?

Imagine the different types of people who might be standing there on the doorstep.

What kind of person would you like to see?

Who would be right to do your hair or care for your child, fix your computer or do your garden?

Draw the type of person you would like to see in your doorway or jot some words to describe your ideal candidate.

You could approach it from the other side and say what would put you off – what would you **not** like to see?

I would **not** want someone who...

You are beginning to understand how it feels to be an employer and how first impressions can give you a good idea about whether someone is going to be suitable or not.

Still, first impressions can be deceptive, so imagine you are willing to invite the person in and give them a chance. Which job are you interviewing them for? Circle one of these...

Hairdresser   Computer person   Childminder   Gardener

Now you have got the person sitting on your sofa or at the kitchen table, or perhaps walking round the garden or looking at your ailing PC. What kind of things will they say and do to persuade you to give the job to them?

☺ They will impress me if they...

What might they say or do to put you off?

☹ I will be put off if they...

Now you know how it feels to be an employer, it is time to consider what the people interviewing you are going to be worrying about.

1. *Can* you do the job?

Are you capable of doing what they need you to do?
- Have you been trained?
- What experience have you had in this sort of work?

Do you know enough about it:
- Theoretical background to the job and recent developments?
- Legislation and other relevant issues?
- About their organisation and how it works?

2. *Will* you do the job?

Will means two things – firstly, can they rely on you?
- Will you turn up every day, at the right time?
- Will you do a good job, every time?
- Will you be there when they need you?

Secondly, are you willing?
- Do you really want this job, are you hungry for it?
- Are you keen and enthusiastic about this sort of work?
- Do you seem passionate about it?

3. Will you *fit in*?

- Will you get on well with other people already there?
- Are you a team player?
- Do you have the image they want to project to customers?
- Do you share the values and vision of the organisation?
- Do they feel comfortable with you, do you like them?

Remember how it feels to be an employer and on the next page, note what you need to do to convince them you...
- **Can** do the job
- **Will** do the job
- **Fit in** to their team, and with their company

The job I am applying for is ……………………………….........

The company is ………………………………………….........

To convince them I **can**	I need to (appear, do, say)...
☆ I am capable of doing this type of work successfully ☆ I have had training ☆ I am experienced in this sort of work ☆ I know sector background, recent developments, legislation and other issues ☆ I know about their organisation	
To convince them I want to	I need to (appear, do, say)...
☆ I'll do a good job, every time ☆ I'll be there when they need me, on time, every time ☆ I'm enthusiastic, passionate about this sort of work ☆ I'm hungry for this job	
To convince them I'll fit in	I need to (appear, do, say)...
☆ I'll get on well with the people already there ☆ I can be a team player ☆ I have the image they want to project to customers ☆ I share the organisation's vision and values ☆ I like them as people, they feel comfortable with me	

Now move on to **TAPAS Step 2** for more help with this.

Step 2   Analyse the Job

When you were wearing the "employer" hat, it was easy to say what sort of person you wanted, because you know yourself and how you feel about things. Now you need to put yourself into the shoes of **this** employer and get a feel for how she or he sees the world. What matters to them? What is important to their organisation? What is this job all about? What do they need from the person in this post?

Analysing the job comes in two stages:

1. gather as much information as you can

2. pick out the most important things this employer needs

Ideally you will narrow the employer's needs down to no more than five or six, and list them. You can use a form like this one on the right.

I think this employer wants someone who...

1. ....

2. ....

3. ....

4. ....

5. ....

If you do not like forms and lists, you can spread your ideas out visually:

Gather Information

Unless you know a bit about this employer and the job, you will not be able to know what they want. So, how can you find out?

Gathering Information – Read the Job Advertisement

Here is an example of one job advertised in the local paper:

COLLEGE GROUNDSPERSON REQUIRED

If you enjoy working outdoors - we have an opportunity for you to help us maintain the grounds and environment of our college. You should be a team worker who also does not mind working alone, well motivated to provide a high standard of work; someone flexible, who enjoys a wide range of tasks and challenges.

Working as a member of the friendly Facilities team, you will be part of a service that maintains the grounds and buildings of the entire college site, providing a safe, clean and welcoming environment for students, staff and visitors.

If this is all the information you are given, you can try to imagine what the employers are looking for. Your five or six points might be...

I think this employer wants someone who...

1. Likes working outdoors

2. Likes working alone but can work in a team

3. Likes variety

4. Is strong, fit and good at practical things

5. Has experience in gardening and building

6. Is friendly and helpful, hardworking, reliable

Gathering Information – Read the Job Description

If it is a large company or organisation with a Human Resources department, you will be sent a Job Description. Job Descriptions give background about the job role, describing what they want you to do and how you will contribute to the organisation's work to help them achieve their goals. This will give you a feel for the company and what is important to them. It will help you think what you can say to you show you will **fit in**.

Job Descriptions can be very long, with a lot of information in them. The newspaper advertisement for the College Groundsperson said that people should send for the detailed job description. Here it is:

HILLTOP COLLEGE	JOB DESCRIPTION: GROUNDSPERSON
ABOUT US:	Hilltop College is a renowned centre of excellence with students from all over the world studying our courses in business management. Summerfield campus is a listed historic building set in five acres of landscaped parkland five miles outside the city.
JOB TITLE:	Grounds Person/Environment Assistant
LOCATION:	Based in the first instance at Summerfield campus, but to work at all premises administered by the Estates & Facilities Division
ACCOUNTABLE TO:	Facilities Manager

JOB PURPOSE
To provide a grounds environmental cleaning service in all outdoor areas and to assist with minor maintenance within the complex. Reporting to Assistant Services Managers, and work in association with Facilities Manager and Estates workforce in delivering a quality focused service. *Cont'd on next page...*

SERVICE DELIVERY

1. To segregate and dispose of household and environmental waste from external waste bins in accordance with College Policy

2. To ensure all entrances, exits, pathways, curb sides and external grids to the premises are maintained in a clean and tidy manner by ensuring that they are free from litter, leaves, grit, snow etc. and providing and maintaining a safe environment for students, staff and the public

3. To assist in cleaning skips and waste collection containers

4. To assist the residences officer on minor maintenance issues and undertake tasks such as:-
   - Changing light bulbs/lampshades
   - Re-hanging doors/drawers and adjusting if required
   - Moving furniture
   - Unblocking sinks

5. To maintain equipment used in course of duties

HEALTH & SAFETY

6. To comply with all health and safety arrangements within area of responsibility including COSHH and the safe storage of chemicals and specialist materials

7. To promptly report any building or equipment defect that could give rise to safety hazards and report and investigate all accidents and untoward incidents

8. To co-operate with and attend training provided for health and safety purposes

9. To maintain requirements for both property and personal safety

PROFESSIONALISM

10. To work flexibly and perform other duties in times of need

11. To promote a professional and positive image

12. To take responsibility for own learning and development and participate fully in appraisal and supervision

Now you have seen the job description, would you make any changes to your list of six things the employer wants? Maybe you got it right the first time, but perhaps you would add to point 4 (Strong, fit and good at practical things) **and able to travel to the site**, because you know it is five miles from the city and some people would find it difficult to get there; and to point 6 (Friendly, helpful, hardworking, reliable) **and professional image**, because you know that their students are international business people and Hilltop College seem very proud of their image. Your list now reads...

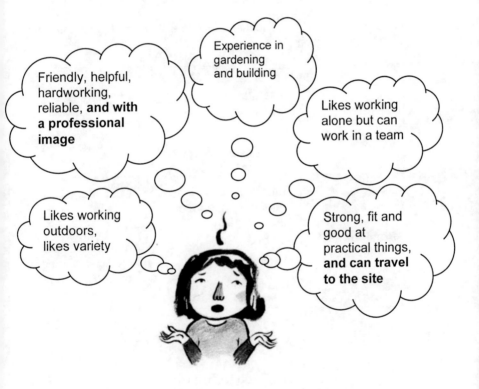

When you reach the next stage "Prepare your Evidence", this extra information about the employer will be very useful.

Gathering Information – Read the Person Specification

If you are sent a Job Description, you will probably also receive one more document that is very important, partly because it has done some of the work for you by analysing what they are looking for – their **criteria**. This document is the Person Specification, which is usually divided into two columns:

| ESSENTIAL criteria | and | DESIRABLE criteria |

Here is the person specification that came with the job description for the groundsperson:

	ESSENTIAL	DESIRABLE
Qualifications **Knowledge**	Understanding and awareness of Health & Safety Entry Level Literacy & Numeracy Skills	NVQ 1 or 2 Risk Awareness
Skills **Previous Experience**	To be able to work as a member of a team or alone To be able to work flexibly Able to work under instruction	Customer service Experience of dealing with members of the public, including business people
Physical Requirements	Good attendance record Ability to perform a wide range of duties according to the Job Description Able to carry out all physical tasks required to fulfil the role	

This person specification is, thank goodness, shorter than the job description. It shows you how the employer is thinking, and although you guessed correctly in several cases, you could add a few points to your list of the employer's key needs. You now know they want a certain level of literacy and numeracy (preferably other relevant qualifications) and that they expect you to understand customer service. So now your list may look like this:

I think this employer wants someone who...

1. Likes working outdoors

2. Likes working alone but can work in a team **and will follow instructions**

3. Likes variety

4. Is strong, fit and good at practical things **and** can travel to the site **and** has **entry level literacy and numeracy skills**

5. Has experience in gardening, building **and customer service**

6. Is friendly, helpful, hardworking, reliable **and** with a professional image **and good attendance**

The job we have used as an example here is a fairly straightforward one. Even so, the job description is still long, although the person specification is short and to the point. The person specification for the post you are applying for may be much longer, with maybe twenty different criteria. Even so, for the interview, it is best to try to pick out no more than six key needs, mainly because you need to be able to remember them and you want to give a strong clear message to the interviewers. As with the Groundsperson position, each of your five or six key needs can combine several similar ones that are listed on the person specification.

The Person Specification and Structured Interviews

If you are sent a person specification, this often means the interview will be structured around it. The interviewers may have a form with all the criteria listed, and will have devised a list of questions aimed at finding out if you meet their criteria. Each candidate will be asked the same questions, and their answers will be scored depending on how well they fit the criteria. This is often called a competency based interview.

So check your list of key needs carefully to make sure everything is included, especially the Essential Criteria - you want to get points for all of them.

No Job Description? How to find out about the company?

You may not get a job description or person specification. This could be because the company is small and informal, without a human resources department – just the owner doing it all himself or herself. Perhaps you sent them your CV "on spec", when no particular job was advertised, and they asked you to come along for a chat. Maybe the interview was arranged through an agency or a friend. Without a written job description, how do you find out about them and what they need?

Gathering Information – Search Online

A quick and easy way to find out about a company is online. Go to your favourite search engine, put in the company's name, and there you have it:

- **The company's own website:**
  - o their **Home page** will show you how they see themselves and how they like to be seen. You can pick up some key words and phrases and use them to create the impression that you are similar to them. This is a tool like "mirroring", which means subtly copying their postures and mannerisms, and using the same language that they use. Note the word "subtle" though!
  - o their **Our Products** or **Our Services** pages will show you what they do. You can get a picture of how your job fits into

their whole enterprise, who their customers are and an idea of what matters to them.

o their **Our People** pages will give you key names, including the head or director of the department you are applying to – it may not yet be clear how you can use this information, but note it just in case.

o their **Contact Us** page will tell you where their head office is, and how many branches they have – this could be useful in helping you understand how you could progress and whether travel will be expected

- **News websites** – has the company been in the news lately? The BBC or national newspapers, specialist magazines, or the local press may tell you something about problems (good to know about though best avoided in interview) or successes – they will love it if you know about these.

- **Blogs and networking sites**[1] may come up in your search – you could learn useful background including a lot of personal opinions about the company. You might learn the background of the actual people interviewing you and what their opinions are on various work issues. One person was able to find out the interviewer had studied at the same college as she had, so she made a point of mentioning her college experience, to spark his interest and help him remember her, as well as create a feeling that, with a similar background, she could fit in with his ideas.

- **Professional bodies** exist for most types of work, with information both for employers and for people in that occupation. Have a look at these, even if you are not a member, and you will learn a lot about what the job involves and what issues are important to the industry at this time. Examples to show the range of occupations that have a professional body:

o The Gardeners Guild

o The Association of Event Organisers

o The Chartered Institute of Logistics and Transport

---

[1] Currently, LinkedIn.com for professional information. For a more informal check, Twitter and Facebook (and remember that they might look for you on Facebook too, so check your profile and privacy settings!)

- **Careers websites** have been set up by the main careers services and describe almost every job role you can think of. Use these to find out the usual duties of the role and what sort of person you need to be – you use this information to add to your list of five or six key things the employer needs. In 2012, some of the UK websites open to all include:
  - o Next Step – www.nextstep.direct.gov.uk
  - o Prospects (graduate careers service) – www.prospects.ac.uk
  - o Careers Scotland – www.careers-scotland.org.uk
  - o Careers Wales / Gyrfa Cymru – www.careerswales.com
  - o NHS Careers – www.nhscareers.nhs.uk

Gathering Information – Ask People

Beware of relying too heavily on the internet. Talking to real people is excellent practice for the interview and there is nothing like networking in person to learn all kinds of subtle information about the company you are aiming for. Ask around. Who is in **your** network?

- Friends
- Family members
- Housemates
- Teachers or College Lecturers
- Work Colleagues
- Careers Advisers, Library Staff
- ... and their friends, parents, partner, brothers and sisters ...

Do you know someone who knows someone who works for the company you are aiming at? Or who does the same kind of job?

Make it a priority to meet them, for a face to face chat if possible or at least a phone call. You may have a list of questions to ask, but you could simply let them tell you about the company or their job, and then listen. Just by listening, you will be picking up a general impression of what makes the company or that profession tick, what is their style and culture, what is important to them, their core values.

You started this section by analysing the job to make a list of six key things the employer needs from the person they appoint to this job.

Then you gathered more information about the job and also about the company. This will be useful, both to help you see how to present yourself so you have the right image, and to show you were keen enough to do some research and find out more about them.

Amy –
rested on her laurels

Amy was approached by Ed, who she knew socially. He owned a local company and he had a vacancy that was ideal for her. Many jobs go through word of mouth and he asked her to pop in for a chat about the job. She knew they got on well together and she had the right skill set. The vacancy hadn't even been advertised. What could go wrong? It was in the bag, surely?

She didn't get the job. Ed was cold called by a job seeker who impressed him deeply with her knowledge of his company and her research about his business sector. She had done her homework well, analysed his needs and put together a compelling case on why she should be hired. Amy, on the other hand, took a casual approach and assumed their friendship was sufficient. She knows better now.

You know better too. You will do your research and when you have gathered enough information you can use the forms on the next few pages to fix it in your mind.

Name of Company or Organisation:

....

o   What do they do or make?

....

o   How many people work there?

....

o   Do they have other branches? Where?

....

o   What is the organisational "culture"? Its values,
     dress code, vision, mission ?

....

o   Who are their customers or target audience?

....

o   What are they famous for, or proud of?

....

The Job or Position I am applying for:

....

o   The Branch, Department, Section or Team?

....

o   The name of the Line Manager?

....

o   What do I know about him/her – management style,
     pet themes, likes, dislikes?

....

o   Who will be interviewing me?

....

Now you are nearly ready to make your perfect list of five or six key things the employer needs from you. Remember that this is to show that:

✓   you **can** do the job

✓   you **will** do the job *and* you really **want** to do the job

✓   you will **fit in**

Think back to when you were imagining looking for a hairdresser or someone to fix your computer. Now remember everything you have found out about this company and this job. Try to put yourself into the employer's shoes and see it from their point of view. What would you need? What would you be afraid of? What kind of person would you be looking for?

Knowing Why

One last thing to help you really understand this employer and their needs, is to know not only what they want but why.

Sometimes it is obvious. If it is an outdoor job, of course they want someone who will be happy working outside. If that person is unhappy outdoors, they will probably leave as soon as an indoor job comes up.

It is not so clear why Hilltop College wants their groundsperson to have a professional image and experience of customer service, until you have learned that the groundsperson comes into contact with the students at this college who are mature business people, accustomed to attending meetings in smart hotels and conference centres. If you can, in your interview, show that you understand why this is important, you will make an even better impression on your interviewers.

Now you are ready to analyse the job you are applying for and complete your list or draw your bubble diagram.

Job .... Employer ....

I think this employer wants someone who...

1. ....

2. ....

3. ....

4. ....

5. ....

6. ....

There is not much room to write on this form. There is a good reason for this – you need to express each of these five or six key needs in a few words that you can remember, perhaps counting them out on the fingers of one hand.

To help you remember them, you might prefer to note them down visually, laying them out like this:

However you decide to list the five or six key requirements of the job, once it is done, leave it alone for a while. Take a walk, make a drink, have a meal or do something different for the rest of the day. After a break, re-read the Job Description and your other research, and look at the list again. Maybe you will make some changes. Once you are happy with the list, you are ready to move on to **TAPAS** step three.

38

Step 3   Prepare your Evidence

How do you persuade someone that you have the ability to do the job they need you to do?

The best way is to give them examples of when you have done it before. It is evidence that they can believe in. You will find this easier to do if you have already thought of things you have done or achieved that are a good examples of the skills they want.

So, for each of the six key things you have decided they need, now try to think of a time when you were in a similar situation and did a good job, resulting in a good outcome for your employer.

Once you have your examples, you can build a story to bring each of them to life, so that those listening can really believe it and picture you in the role.

Telling your story has another very useful purpose. As you concentrate on describing what happened, you will forget your nerves and start to relax. As you think back to an event where you did well and achieved a successful outcome, you will relive the experience and this will affect your body language. It will become that of a confident, successful and enthusiastic person. As they listen, the interviewers will be see a competent person and be able to imagine you performing like that in their company.

First, decide on a story that will demonstrate your ability to meet each of the employer's six key needs.

For each key need, think of a time when you showed the qualities and skills they need. Choose a time when...

- you helped get a good result
- you saved the situation
- you solved a problem
- you created something new
- you made or saved money

List your stories in this table.

The Employer needs someone who …	This story will show I have done this before …
Copy from your list on page 36	Give each story a short title that will jog your memory
1.	
2.	
3.	
4.	
5.	
6.	

Team leader Chris was applying for an office manager position and had to show the ability to *Motivate a team and get the best out of them.* Chris decided to tell the story of "How I motivated a nervous new member of staff, Annie" and gave the story a short, memorable title "Anxious Annie".

The Employer needs someone who can...	This story will show I have done this before...
Motivate their team and get the best out of them	*Anxious Annie*

Now Chris has to make sure the story comes across convincingly.

Be a STAR!

Tell your STAR story

S.T.A.R. is a four-step structure to make sure you keep your story brief, interesting and to the point. Here is how Chris might tell the story of Anxious Annie, demonstrating the ability to *motivate a team and get the best out of them.*

SITUATION
Describe the Situation where this happened – Set the Scene

In my job as team leader at Brooks, we took on a new member of staff. We all have to use a specially designed spreadsheet.

TASK
Say what needed to be done, the problem to be solved

This new person was very nervous about using it. She believed it was all maths and she thought she couldn't do it. It was very important to persuade her to learn this, as we were short staffed and needed her to take her share of the work.

ACTIONS
Describe what YOU did, say I, not we

I believed she had the ability and just lacked confidence. I gave her a task that I knew she could handle, and I sat with her at first. I didn't help her unless she asked, and I praised her every time she got it right. I designed step by step a series of tasks that taught her all she needed to know without her realising it.

RESULT
Describe the result of your action – how it was good for the company

She is now so keen on the system that she wants to use it all the time. She is one of our most efficient team members and I've just given her an extra responsibility of teaching it to new people.

Now, draft notes* for your 1st STAR story

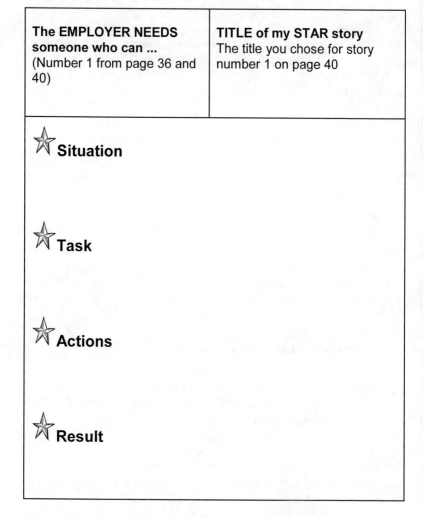

The EMPLOYER NEEDS someone who can ... (Number 1 from page 36 and 40)	TITLE of my STAR story The title you chose for story number 1 on page 40

⭐ **Situation**

⭐ **Task**

⭐ **Actions**

⭐ **Result**

* Just notes, not whole sentences. You are not going to read from this sheet, because you want to sound natural. The notes are just to help you remember so they need to be short and sweet.

Do practise this at home

When you have thought how you will tell the story, you really need to practise. Find a helpful friend or relative who will listen, and tell your story. Give it all you have got, and tell it proudly, reliving the big moment as you tell it. Then ask for encouraging but honest feedback.

If there were bits they did not understand or follow, you can go back and tweak it.

If you really cannot find anyone to listen to you, you could try speaking your STAR story aloud to yourself. Better would be to record it, then listen and be your own critical friend. However, a real live audience is best – and more fun!

Once you are happy with STAR story number one, move on to the next. You have four or five more to prepare.

Once you have made your list of the employer's five or six key needs and prepared a STAR story for each, you can use them in lots of situations. Interviewers often like to ask very general, open questions. Any of these questions could be answered by listing the five or six key requirements or choosing one and telling its STAR story.

Why do you want this job?

Tell me about yourself.

What are you good at?

What makes you think you can do this job?

What sort of person are you?

What are your strengths?

Tell us about something you are proud of.

If you were applying for the groundsperson position, you could answer like this:

1.   Why do you want this job?

> I'd love this job as it seems so suitable for me
>
> I am working at a garden centre so am used to (key need) **helping customers**, but I am really a (key need) **practical** person and would rather spend more time (key need) **outdoors**.
>
> ✲ I've been a conservation volunteer for two years at a local nature reserve so I know how to use ✲**horticultural** machinery to keep grass and bushes tidy, and **woodworking and** ✲**construction** tools to repair fences, paths, and buildings.

By answering the question, you have been able to show you can meet at least three of their needs. You could give a very similar answer to all the other open questions.

2.   Tell me about yourself.

3.   Why should we take you on?

4.   What are you good at?

5.   What makes you think you can do this job?

6.   What sort of person are you?

7.   What are your strengths?

8.   Tell us about something you are proud of

This last question gives you the chance to focus on one of their needs and tell one of your STAR stories, giving them a lot more detail so that they begin to get to know you.

You can choose any one of their needs. For example, one applicant might focus on "Friendly, helpful, hardworking, reliable, with a professional image". Here is their STAR story sheet:

The EMPLOYER NEEDS someone who can ... (Number 6 from page 29)	**TITLE of my STAR story** The title this person chose to tell for story number 6
Friendly, helpful, hardworking, reliable, with a professional image	*Disabled customer last Christmas*

 Situation

Garden Centre, Last Christmas, Busy, Stressed out

 Task

Man on sticks, stuck in crowd – I was on another errand

⭐ **Actions**

Tactfully offered help, persuaded a customer to assist

⭐ **Result**

Didn't offend anyone, helped disabled person in need, a very satisfied customer, area manager commendation

If there were asked "Tell us about something you are proud of", they might actually tell the story like this:

Situation

I was very proud of a letter my manager received from a customer. It was last Christmas at the garden centre. It was very busy and crowded, and I'd kept smiling all day even when some customers had been quite impatient and rude. There was pressure on us to work fast and get them served as quickly as possible.

Task

As I went to the shelves to find a different size drill for a customer waiting at the cash desk, I noticed a man walking with difficulty on two sticks, trying to get into the queue but being pushed to the side by the other customers. I wanted to help but they were waiting for me at the till.

Action

I went up to him and quietly asked if he was trying to get into the queue – I was careful not to assume he wanted help, as I didn't want to be pushy. He said Yes, looking quite upset.

I couldn't stay with him because they were waiting for me at the till, so I spotted a friendly looking person in the queue and gently pointed out that this gentleman was trying to get in. Once they noticed, they apologised and let him in front of them. On my way back to the till, I saw them chatting together and the man on sticks looked much happier.

Result

I was pleased that I managed to get the man into the queue without offending either him or the person I asked to help.

Also, I didn't keep my colleague waiting at the till for the replacement drill for too long.

The customer wrote a thank you note to my manager. He showed it to his area manager and got a commendation for giving the company a good reputation as disability friendly.

That was a STAR story to answer the interviewer's request to "tell us something you are proud of". This very open type of question gives you the chance to choose one of the key requirements you had identified and tell a STAR story of your choice.

Often the questions will be more specific, giving you less choice. The employer may choose one of their own requirements and ask for an example, with "Tell us about a time when you ...". If you have done a good job of analysing their needs, you may well have a STAR story ready prepared. You could use the story about customer service to answer: Tell us about a time when you...

- provided excellent customer service
- showed diplomacy skills
- contributed towards your company's good reputation
- acted in support of equality and diversity laws
- went the extra mile
- persuaded someone to do something
- avoided a crisis by good negotiation

To be on the safe side, especially where you have been given a person specification, you can prepare a STAR story for every point in the list of Essential Criteria. If there are too many of these, why not just look at your five or six key STAR stories, and see if you can weave in to one or other of them something to show each point. One

STAR story can be used as evidence for several key needs at the same time.

Your STAR stories do not have to be about things you did at work. The person applying for the groundsperson post included (page 44) examples from their voluntary work. This will be especially important if you have recently left school or university or if you are changing career direction, as your work experience might not have provided opportunities to do work at the right level.

We have helped people prepare job applications and interviews using examples from their personal life and their voluntary work. Some of these were:

- serving as a local parish councillor
- anti-bullying peer buddy at school
- organising a fund-raising concert
- coaching an under-14s football team
- running a local street arts festival
- helping in their child's classroom
- writing film reviews for their film club's website
- serving at a soup kitchen
- caring for a sick relative
- campaigning to get a skateboard park built

So, think widely about all the different things you take part in, at all times of day and in all aspects of your life, and choose for your STAR stories the achievements that most closely match the skills and the attitudes needed for the job.

When you have prepared at least five (maybe more) STAR stories, you will be ready for **TAPAS step 4.**

But first, a danger story.

 Bob – not a boy scout

A tool hire company were interviewing for a trainee team leader role. They wanted someone with potential who they could train up to grow into the role. Bob had recently graduated as a mature student, following a long period of unemployment. The panel were impressed that he taken steps to improve his employability, so they interviewed him.

Unfortunately, Bob's answers soon fell into a pattern. He was asked about teams he had played a part in, problems he had solved, how he would cope with work based challenges – all pretty standard questions. Bob's reply to every one was a variation of "I can't think of an example right now..." He started the interview with goodwill from the panel, but his lack of preparation soon changed that.

The scout's motto is Be Prepared. With your carefully planned STAR stories, you will not fall into the same trap as Bob did.

Step 4 Adjust to Fit

Now for something a bit different. For **TAPAS Steps 2** and **3** you had to be logical and organised, analysing the job, picking out the employer's key needs and then choosing STAR stories for your evidence. Now you need to look at the other side of being interviewed, which has more to do with feelings and emotions.

All of us make up our minds about things in two ways. Sometimes we can be very logical, weighing up and pro's and cons, gathering and analysing the evidence:

> "What time shall I go to bed this evening? I need to be up early in the morning, I've got an important job interview, I need my sleep to perform well – so I'll be in bed by 11."

At other times, we forget about logic and let our feelings dictate:

> "I've got an important job interview in the morning, I feel scared, I don't want to think about it, and there's a repeat of my favourite film on TV, I'll just stay up for the beginning – oh, I watched it all and now it's 1 am."

- **Adjust your Image**

Interviewers also use both head and heart to make up their minds. They can look at all the evidence that says you will be perfect for their job role, but if you walk into the room looking different from what they expect, their hearts will say No even if their head says Yes. You may need to adjust your image, so their hearts will say Yes too.

- **Adjust your Mindset**

Feelings will also affect your performance. Sometimes we can be fully prepared for something – a driving test, an exam, a sports match or an interview. But on the day, our nerves take over, our confidence melts away and we flop. You may need to adjust your feelings, your mindset, to build yourself up and perform at your best.

TAPAS Step 4 shows how to make these two adjustments.

Adjusting your Image

Do you remember **TAPAS Step 1** when you tried to get inside the interviewer's head and think like an employer?

You imagined choosing a hairdresser, a childminder or someone to help you with your computer or your garden. You imagined the ring on the doorbell, opening your front door and – what do you see?

Research has shown two interesting things about the effect of what you see. First, look at this chart.

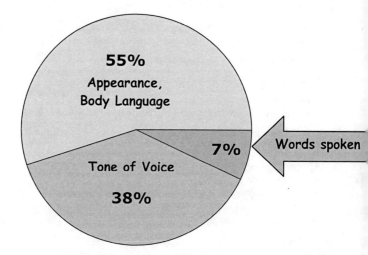

It represents research[2] that shows what you will have noticed in everyday life. If someone says "it's lovely to see you" or "I like your shoes" you know whether they mean it or not. How do you know? Probably because you see the expression on their face, the way they are standing, and you feel warmth (or not) in their voice.

According to this research, all the words you say during the interview – including the STAR stories you have carefully prepared – will only count for 7% of the impression you make on the hearts of your

[2]by Albert Mehrabian, see last section "Read more about it".

interviewers, even though your words are also essential to appeal to their logical heads.

Blink! First Impressions

The second piece of relevant research says that all of us instinctively make up our mind about many things, especially about people, in the time it takes to blink once! "Blink"[3] is the title of a whole book illustrating this point. The research goes on to say that once we make that first blink of an eye judgement, we filter everything that happens later, tending to only take notice of evidence that backs up our first impression.

Is this good news for job applicants? Is there any point in carefully analysing the employer's needs and preparing STAR stories if the interviewers make up their minds within a split second of seeing you?

Yes, because people decide with their heart and their head. Trained interviewers conducting structured interviews know that the instinctive "Blink!" decision is not reliable enough. They will still feel what their heart tells them but they will take more notice of their head.

Not all interviews are so structured, especially in smaller organisations where staff selection is only done occasionally by the manager or business owner. It may be a job they find difficult and want to get over as quickly as possible. If they have had no interview training, they might be more influenced by gut feelings, their heart.

To be on the safe side, you need to cover both angles. Make sure the image the interviewer sees in their "Blink!" moment tells them that you are right for the job and also have STAR stories prepared to back up that first impression with hard evidence.

So, how should you look? What should they see in their "Blink!" moment as you walk into the interview room? Look at the images on the next two pages then read on and answer some questions.

---

[3]by Malcolm Gladwell, see last section "Read more about it".

What do you
think?

What first impression would each of these people make?

Which ones look the most...

- ☐ Friendly?
- ☐ Competent?
- ☐ Cheerful?
- ☐ Good at their job?
- ☐ Fun?
- ☐ Easy to get on with?
- ☐ Helpful, co-operative?
- ☐ Patient with difficult people?
- ☐ Trustworthy?

- ☐ Assertive?
- ☐ Energetic?
- ☐ Successful?
- ☐ Influential?
- ☐ Caring?
- ☐ Reliable?
- ☐ Professional?
- ☐ Managerial?
- ☐ Creative?
- ☐ Enthusiastic?

Who looks like a...

- ☐ Hairdresser?
- ☐ Gardener?
- ☐ Supervisor?
- ☐ Lawyer?
- ☐ Software engineer?
- ☐ Manager?
- ☐ Pre-school teacher?

- ☐ Social Worker?
- ☐ Merchant banker?
- ☐ Engineering apprentice?
- ☐ Accountant?
- ☐ Customer Service Adviser?
- ☐ Airline pilot?
- ☐ Management consultant?

...and who does not?

What made you think that? Was it their...

- o Facial expression?
- o Posture?
- o Hairstyle?
- o Clothes?
- o Grooming?
- o Accessories?
- o or something else...?

Look and Feel

The questions on the previous page are simply about the visual impression you get from a small drawing. If you open the door to someone or if they walk into the room where you are sitting, your short "Blink!" will take in a bit more than you get from a drawing. What might you notice and then process instantly to arrive at your first "Blink!" impression?

o   The way they walk into the room – lively, confident, uncertain?

o   The way they look at you – anxious, frowning, friendly, respectful, hostile?

o   The way they move – twitchy, calm, stiff, smooth, slow?

o   How quickly they respond to what you say?

o   How they respond – smile, laugh, eager nod, a word or two?

o   Their scent – neutral, overpowering, fashionable, cheap?

o   Their handshake – taking the initiative, waiting for your first move, unprepared, limp, bone-crushing?

o   The way they sit down – awkward, easily, clumsy, slouching?

These are more about the atmosphere they create and the way they make you feel. Do you think they admire you? Or do you feel they are slightly critical or superior, giving the impression they know everything and are here to impose their views on you? All of these small actions will give you an impression of them, the kind of job they do, what type of company they work for and how they treat other people.

Of course, the next step is to turn this round and look at yourself. What will the interviewer see and feel as **you** walk through the door? Go right now to a full length mirror. Look honestly, as others might see you, and rate yourself against the checklist on the previous page.

Now, how do you **want** to come across when you walk into that interview room? Do you need to make any changes?

Mirror image – dress for where you want to be

Aisha was working as an administrator for a city legal firm when she came for career guidance. She was neatly groomed, in fashionable office clothes and shoes, wearing make-up, lipstick, and varnished nails, with perfectly styled and coloured hair. The look was businesslike and efficient.

She wanted a change of career, and after much thought she decided to become a teacher. She went off to university in another town.

At the end of the year she came back to report on how she was getting on. A different person walked into the office. Still fashionable, but more casual, with bubbly hair, arty scarf, jeans and flat shoes. Now she looked like a student teacher, more creative and informal, and it was easy to imagine her teaching a class of young children.

Aisha had understood how to adapt her look to fit the image of her chosen career.

Organisations and professions have their own culture, which is often obvious through their dress and grooming. City legal firms want to project a serious, professional and efficient image to demanding business customers. Schools are often more down to earth places, where you have to manage groups of lively children, maybe rolling up your sleeves and getting your hands dirty. If Aisha went for an interview at her old firm dressed in her student teacher style, you can guess the reaction.

It is also possible to be too smart. High heels and painted nails would look out of place in a primary school and turning up there for interview so smartly dressed could give the impression that she was not robust and flexible enough for the demands of that job.

So getting back to you and the job you are aiming for, how do you need to look if you are dressing for the place you want to be?

Circle the words that apply to the job role you are applying for:

Professional   Intelligent   Approachable   Capable   Tough

Creative   Persuasive   Strong   Sensitive   Gentle   Serious

Trustworthy   Fashionable   Warm and Caring   Successful

Down to Earth   Influential   Fit and Active   Up to date[4]

In the mirror, make some notes or draw a picture to emphasise how **you** need to look in order to present the right image for the job you want.

Think about...
- Haircut
- Hair style
- Jacket
- Suit
- Tie
- Shirt
- Clean
- Ironed
- Hair colour
- Make-up
- Shoes
- Heels

Think about...
- Glasses
- Jewellery
- Bare flesh
- Tights
- Trousers
- Jeans
- Bag
- Briefcase
- Coat
- Teeth
- Posture
- Perfume

[4] Some coaches use the word **Contemporary**. You do not have to be in the latest fashions but if your style is too out of date, it can give the impression that you are out of touch professionally as well.

Dressing for where you want to be is achievable if you already know something about the company and have a clear picture of the image that will impress them. If you do not, you need to do some research. Check the notes you made for **TAPAS Step 2**.

John was a park ranger and always went to work in clothes that could stand all weathers and were suitable for manual work. If he had to attend a meeting in the office he would leave his muddy boots at the door, but otherwise stay dressed the same.

He got an interview for an area manager post in a government environmental department, based at their head office.

"I didn't know what to wear. In the job I'd still go out visiting nature reserves, so a smart business suit would be ridiculous. But as this interview was for a manager's position, maybe they expected a suit.

"I phoned my old college tutor and asked what he knew about the organisation. He sent me their latest annual report which had some photos of managers. Now I knew – jacket and tie, but country colours, not a city suit. I had the right thing at home, and when I walked into the interview room, I felt I fitted in well."

Too sexy for the role?

Jenny went for an interview to work in a care home. Another applicant was a woman wearing stilettos and a tight pencil skirt. Jenny's heart sank as she compared herself with this smart, confident woman, although she couldn't imagine her gently caring for elderly residents! The employers rang that evening and offered Jenny the job. They obviously agreed with her assessment. Remember – dress for the role you want.

Adjusting your Mindset

Now you have decided how you want to appear at the "Blink!" moment when the interviewers see you for the first time. You know how to find out more about the "look" of people who work there, so you can adjust your image to fit.

Having adjusted your image, you are dressed for the part. That is exactly what you will be doing – playing a part, acting a role. We all play several roles in our lives. This book focuses on our role as a worker but at times we may also have the role of friend, partner, carer, follower, leader, student, teacher, child or parent. We may behave like quite different people in each of these roles. You would act very differently with a young child you that are looking after in the morning from how you would in a meeting that same afternoon to discuss a loan with the bank manager.

To convince the interviewers you are right for their role, you have thought carefully about what they will see in their "Blink!" moment when they first meet you. The visual impression you create is the first, very important thing to work on.

There is more, however. Acting a role is not just about the costume but also about how you stand, move and speak. In the first moment when the interviewers meet you and throughout the interview too, they must be able to imagine you in the role of the person they need. They have to feel confident that you are the kind of person who can do the job effectively in the way they want it done.

How can you help them to visualise you in the role? You have enough to think about already without having to remember another set of do's and don'ts. You could try a few of these tools:

- **Modelling**
- **Method Acting**
- **Passion**
- **Visualisation**
- **Treasure Chest**
- **Self Talk**

Modelling

Matt came to see Ann because he had attended several interviews for lecturing posts but had not got the job. Now he had found one he really wanted, in just the right kind of school with a good reputation. He had excellent references from his training placements and he knew he was a good teacher, but he had not been able to put this across at interview.

He agreed to do a practice interview with me. I could see immediately what the problem was. He sidled into the room, sat stiffly in his seat, looked down at his feet and answered my questions with one or two words only. Based on that performance, I could not imagine any group of students taking much notice of him.

Our conversation at the end of the practice session went like this:

Matt   That's what always happens. I get so nervous I just can't relax and be myself.

Ann   How would you like to appear when you walk into the interview?

Matt   Friendly, outgoing, knowledgeable – confident!

Ann   Do you know anyone who would act as you'd like to?

Matt (brightening up) Antony! He's one of our mates, he's really confident – he's bright, intelligent, he's always got something to say, he's lively and fun and got a real presence.

Ann   Try walking into the room again and, just for fun, pretend to be Antony. Walk in like he would.

What a transformation! A different person came into the room, full of energy, standing up straight, looking me in the eye, smiling and positive, and then sat down and answered the questions fully, giving lots of detailed STAR story examples of things he had achieved with his students. He was as delighted as I was with his performance and a week later I got a call to say he had got the job he wanted.

Rather than try to remember lots of instructions "head up, eye contact, smile, speak up, relax", Matt just had to say two words to himself before he walked in: "Be Antony". If nerves are stopping you performing at your best, who are you going to model yourself on as you walk in to the interview? Who are you going to be?

My model is ....

As I walk in the door,

I'll walk in like ....

Modelling a confident friend or family member can help you appear confident yourself, even if you do not want to model them throughout the interview. It is quite possible that Antony would not be a good college lecturer, so keeping up the modelling would give the wrong impression. What it has done is put Matt into the mindset to walk into the room with a confidence that says to the interviewers in their "Blink!" moment: "This person knows his subject. He can command attention and put it across to bright students in an interesting way".

What happens next is that the interviewers respond to this confident person and Matt picks up their positive feelings. Confidence feeds off itself. If in the "Blink!" moment he had disappointed the interviewers by creating the impression of someone timid and quiet, the interviewers' disappointment would have bounced back to him and made him feel he had failed. A downward spiral. This time, because he impressed them in their "Blink!" moment, he picked up their positive response. This fed his confidence and he could perform at his best. It became an upward spiral.

You can use modelling for more than that crucial "Blink!" moment. What if you are going for a promotion, perhaps to team manager, and you need to project the image of someone in a role you have never experienced? They may ask you a "scenario" question:

- **What would you do if** two people didn't get on and their relationship was upsetting the rest of the team?
- **What would you do if** someone kept taking time off sick and you suspected they were not ill?

If you know a manager who is good at their job, you could think of that person as you answer and say to yourself "I am answering like Jane would", or even "Be Jane". As you answer, you will sit and speak like Jane does so that your whole bearing is that of a competent, confident manager.

Method Acting

There was a time in the theatre when acting had become very stylised and wooden. Actors would speak their lines with a lot of noise and extravagant gestures but very little genuine feeling, so that the effect was unrealistic and left the audience unmoved. The actors were modelling the outward behaviour of their characters, but still something was missing.

The concept of method acting, in a (very small) nutshell, asked actors to feel at first hand the emotions of the character they were playing. The technique required them to go back to a time when they had felt that emotion in their own life, and to relive it. By truly experiencing the feelings, they would bring the character to life and would make the drama so much more real for the audience.

You can use this technique to make your story real for your audience, to really convince your interviewers that you are right for the job. If you want to show you are a confident leader, you need to think back to an occasion when you were leading people and it was working well. Method acting asks you to remember everything that was going on for you in that moment, asking for details like:

- where were you standing or sitting?
- how hard was the ground beneath your feet, or the chair you were sitting on?
- how warm or cold was it?
- what could you feel, smell around you?
- what sounds were in the background?
- who were you with? where were they in the room in relation to you?
- how did you feel: how were you standing, how were your feet positioned, which muscles were tense, how were your shoulders, chest, how were you breathing, what were your hands doing?
- how were people responding to you?

Thinking back in this kind of detail to how you felt in that moment when you were performing at your best and getting so much appreciation makes you live it again and give off an aura of success that they cannot help responding to.

Passion

Recruiters love the word "passion". They not only want someone who **can** do the job, **wants** to do the job and **will fit in** to the team and the company's image, they also ask for "**someone who is passionate about**" what they do (children's rights, excellent customer service, saving the planet, strong leadership, etc.).

What are you
passionate about?

Think of a time when you felt especially strongly about this, and see if you can make a STAR story out of it. It will be even better if your STAR story is relevant to one of the employer's key needs.

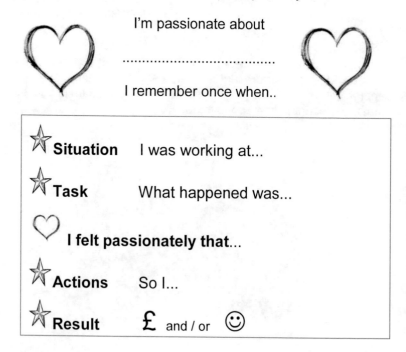

I'm passionate about

....

I remember once when..

⭐ **Situation**   I was working at...

⭐ **Task**   What happened was...

♡ **I felt passionately that**...

⭐ **Actions**   So I...

⭐ **Result**   £ and / or ☺

Visualisation

One of the benefits of having some STAR stories in your mind is to take you back emotionally to successful moments, so that you can relive the good feelings. As well as helping you illustrate one of your key qualities, they make you feel more confident and passionate as they take you back to moments when everything went right.

Sports people are taught to use visualisation not only to remember past events but also to imagine the future. A tennis player will focus on his semi-final against the world number one. He has to overcome the feeling that this person has won many times before and is unbeatable. This is a self-defeating thought. To overcome it, he must replace it with a positive vision.

The coach asks him to visualise the day of the match. He has to visualise winning a point, playing a brilliant shot. He is asked to describe in detail (in the present tense) what is happening:

Visualise placing a shot out of the reach of your opponent...
- what are you thinking as you go to hit the ball?
- where are you aiming to put it?
- what does it sound like as you hit the ball square on the racket?

Follow the ball with your eyes as it goes into the corner out of your opponent's reach...
- what does he do?
- what are the crowd doing?
- what does it sound like?
- how do you feel now?

People who have to make a speech in public often use this method of visualising how the audience respond to their interesting and passionate presentation. You can use it too, to visualise how the interviewers will look impressed as you walk confidently into the room, take your seat like a professional, listen carefully and respond clearly to their questions.

Try to visualise:

- the interviewers looking pleased and satisfied as you complete yet another STAR story, having remembered to finish with your punch line: "and as a result..."

- the moment when they say "We'd like to offer you the job"

  - What is the look on their faces?
  - How are they sitting, standing?
  - How do you feel at this moment?
  - How are you breathing?
  - What are you looking at? What can you see?
  - Which part of your body are you aware of?
  - How does it feel as you hear the words:

Treasure Chest

Building up a collection of treasure is something you can start today. The treasure is anything that makes you feel good about yourself, that gives you a warm glow of confidence, and reminds you "Yes, I have got skills", "Yes, people think I'm OK!"

People have put all kinds of things into their treasure chest:

Azad: My **Clubman of the Year trophy**. I was smaller than the other lads in my team and not very good at football. But I was voted Clubman of the Year because I came to every match and every training even if I spent whole matches on the subs bench sometimes. They said I'm a brilliant team player.

Annie: **Feedback forms** from the first training course I ran. People were really happy with it. I especially like what one man wrote, he was a teacher himself. He said he had enjoyed the course, I'd made it very interesting and adapted to the wide range of abilities in the group. That made me feel so good, it was what I had been trying to do.

Dave: **A card with a note on it** of something one of my managers said. I hadn't known what he thought of me, but one day a manager from another department passed us in the corridor and told him about a problem he was having getting an event organised. My manager said: *'Dave's the man you want, he's a genius at organisation'*. I felt so proud.

Jody: "**A photo** of the family I babysat for all through secondary school. The children said I was their favourite babysitter as I was such good fun, and the mum and dad said they never worried when I was in charge, I was so responsible and competent, especially for someone so young."

Michael: The **leaving card** they gave me when our factory closed and I was made redundant. It's one of those really big ones and it's covered with warm wishes, funny drawings and thanks for the way I had managed the team and helped individual people through difficulties. When I'm feeling low, it really gives me a boost.

Most people's treasure chest is not actually a chest. It could be a box file or ring binder, or a shoe box. If you have not already got one, please do find one and start putting all those morale boosters into it. They really help when you are feeling low, and they will give you quotes to say to yourself as you are about to enter the interview room.

Self Talk

No, it is not a sign that you are losing the plot, though you might choose a time and place where you will not be overheard talking to yourself.

Self talk is a technique encouraged in NLP – neuro-linguistic programming. The theory is that we can programme our mindset (that is the "neuro" bit) with the words we say (the "linguistics" or language we use).

First, get a few sticky notes, say about five or six. Then think of five or six things you need to really believe about yourself, to help you perform well at the interview. They can be general things about you as a person:

Since the purpose of this exercise is to prepare you for a job interview, you might like to add some of your key qualities that will be needed for the position:

> I am a hugely **successful salesman** who has achieved consistently good results.

> I am a highly **creative graphic designer**. My designs have put my firm at the top of its league.

> I am an **excellent communicator**. I can help people understand complicated things.

Having written your strong points carefully, in your best handwriting (you are proud of them, so you will do them the honour of presenting them well) you need to stick them up on a mirror that you use every morning. If you do not want anyone else to know what you are doing and you share your bathroom, you can always put them up each morning and then take them down to use again the next day.

Every morning, look yourself in the eye in the mirror and read out each of the statements in a strong, clear voice. The theory says you have to repeat this every morning, for at least 21 days. After 21 consecutive days, you should be programmed!

What will your sticky notes say?

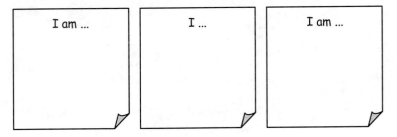

> I am ...

> I ...

> I am ...

A good example of the power of repeating a simple phrase is the three-word statement that Barack Obama used during the run-up to the US presidential elections in 2008. By repeating it so often, you could say he was programming his supporters to believe they could win and that it was worth going out to vote.

He said: You will say:

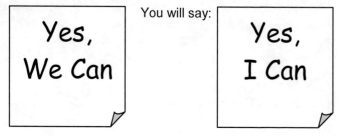

Try to mirror the expression on his face and the way he stood while he said it. You probably can remember it – see the power of repetition?

Talking of phrases we hear over and over, here is another to say...

Please speak this out loud, now!

Repeat every day, for 21 days, spoken out loud and clear!

If you do not have 21 days before the interview, do it twice or three times a day, until you have said *Yes I Can* 21 times.

When you're smiling

Julie's story: I arrived at my first interview for a post teaching adults, well prepared but very conscious of my lack of relevant qualifications, and with a whole lot of nerves. I had taken my friend Sue with me to look after my toddler while I was in the interview, leaving them both in a nearby coffee shop. Just before I left them Sue confided that she had fallen for my friend Carl, but was too shy to approach him. The night before, Carl had told me he had a crush on Sue but thought she wouldn't be interested in him. Dear reader, to cut a long story short, they married.

The reason for telling you this is that it completely altered my mood. My nerves disappeared and I went into the interview smiling, happy about the turn of events. I'm sure my new found *joie de vivre* helped – and getting that job was crucial in shaping my career. I was lucky. You can't rely on a happy event occurring at just the right time, but you can bring one to mind to focus on if your nerves are taking over.

That story illustrates what adjusting your mindset is all about. It really does make a difference to how you appear to your interviewers.

Now you are ready for the big day itself, and **TAPAS Step 5** will show you how to put it all together and give your star performance.

Step 5 Shine like a STAR

Now comes the moment you have been preparing for. All the thinking, analysing and self talk have done their job. You understand how the employers feel and you know what they need. You have the evidence to prove you are what they are looking for and you know how to explain it using STAR stories. You have dressed for the part and adjusted your mindset to act the role and be confident. The thinking is over and it is time to act.

Think ahead to the day itself. We are going to think about the interview in three stages – the beginning, the middle and the end.

Beginning   **Middle**   **End**

What does this mean? You remember the "Blink!" moment. The first moment the interviewers set eyes on you is the one they will remember most strongly. The research goes on to say that they also remember the last few minutes fairly well, and the bit in the middle tends to get forgotten – unless you work extra hard to make it memorable. In this section we will give you some ideas for how to shine at every stage, so they will remember you as a star throughout.

The Beginning

You have read **TAPAS Step 4** and adjusted both your image and your mindset to look and feel the part, the role you are aiming for, and to look and feel confident. You know that first "Blink!" moment is all-important and you are ready to walk in, full of self belief, warmth and confidence. You have some self talk ringing in your ears:

and the other notes that you stuck round the mirror and repeated daily. You have chosen your role model to walk in the door thinking:

I'll walk in as if I was.....................................

Now, as you stand outside the door ready to make your entrance, prepare to make the most of your "Blink!" moment. You must get your body in good working order so you have maximum impact. Here are three things to tell yourself just before you walk into the room:

1. **Deep Breath**
2. **Eye Contact**
3. **Smile**

Deep Breath

Your deep breath is for energy, so you can walk in with an enthusiastic spring in your step. Taking a deep breath as you walk through the door will give you a confident posture. It will make you stand up tall with your chest forward, your shoulders down and back.

Eye Contact

Your eye contact is to show you are interested in them. If there is more than one person in the room, move your eyes round to each in turn, to include everyone.

Smile

Your smile is to make them feel good, that you are happy to be here talking with them. It will move round with the eye contact to each person in turn.

So far, so good, you have probably got past the "Blink!" moment. But you are still quite near the beginning and the impression you make now will still be one they hold on to, so there are three more things to do:

4. **Relax**
5. **Listen**
6. **Respond**

and then one more:

7. **Respect**

Relax

By this time, you might have tensed up, so you need to remember not to overdo the energy, and relax so that they feel relaxed with you. Are your shoulders still down or have they crept up towards your ears? Push those shoulders down, take another breath in, keep smiling, keep eye contact. Feel warmth for these people – you like them, they are OK. Keep your breath slow and deep.

Listen

While you control your breathing it gives you time to listen, really listen. When we are nervous it is very easy to miss what is being said to us and if we do not hear, we cannot give the right response.

Respond

People like to feel listened to, so you need to show you are listening. How do you know whether or not someone is really listening to what you say? They probably look at you, nod in the right places and maybe smile, laugh or say "Mmm" or "Yes". So if you can give these small, non-verbal responses, you will increase the good feelings they get about you. It will also help you to concentrate, so that you understand what they are saying and can give the right response when the time comes.

Respect

This is the last in your list of "On the Day" instructions, but it is an important psychological tool in your toolkit. We are told interviews are supposed to be two-sided, as much for you to find out whether you want the job as for them to decide if they want you. This is true in principle, but in most cases the power balance in an interview situation is not equal. They have a job to offer and you (probably) want it. At least, you want to be offered it. So the interviewers have to feel good about you.

The person who is going to line manage you will almost certainly be one of the interviewers and that person has to feel the relationship will work. You have to strike a balance. The manager must believe you know your job well, that you are competent and confident. But they must also believe you will take a lead from them and be happy to work for them. They are already there, in position, and you are coming new on to their patch, their territory.

It is rather like going to visit someone in their home. You would let them show you into the room and where to sit. They decide the order of the day, what will happen when. You would not criticise their decor or get into an argument with them, because there is an unspoken agreement that on their territory you will let them be in charge. You will probably take your cue from them about when to leave and you will thank them for a nice day.

So, your Memo note to help you shine on the day has seven points:

1. **Deep Breath**
2. **Eye Contact**
3. **Smile**
4. **Relax**
5. **Listen**
6. **Respond**
7. **Respect**

And always ...   **Be Confident**

The Middle

The picture on page 75 shows that people pay less attention to what happens in the middle of a meeting. But please do not be fooled into thinking it does not matter what happens between the first "Blink!" moment and the final good-byes. If you have made a good first impression, your interviewers will be in the right mood to value what you have to say, but you still need to work at giving your evidence and keeping their attention.

Giving your Evidence – Questions and STAR Stories

You cannot guess exactly what questions they will ask but you have worked through **TAPAS Steps 1-4**. Armed with your STAR stories and your analysis of the employer's key needs, you should be ready to respond to anything they ask you. You will try to work out which of their needs (criteria) they are focusing on with each question and you will choose relevant STAR stories to show you can meet each one.

No one can prepare for every possible question and they might ask something you have not prepared for. Your practice in choosing and telling STAR stories will still be useful. You will find it much easier to think on the spot of a suitable one and you now know how to structure each story into four parts:
* Situation
* Task
* Action
* Result

In the next section "What if…?" you will find some more hints on how to deal with the unexpected during the interview.

Keeping their Attention

This middle section of the interview will start well, thanks to your star entrance. As the timeline diagram shows, they will start to lose concentration as time goes on, so you have to work hard to stop their attention wandering. How do you keep a story interesting? Here are some hints:

KISS – sounds fun! It just stands for **K**eep **I**t **S**hort and **S**imple.

The key word here has to be **Short**. Your whole STAR story should not last longer than four minutes, and two minutes would be even better. That means :

☆ Set the Scene – 30-60 seconds

☆ Describe the Task or Problem – 30-60 seconds

☆ Describe your Actions – 30-60 seconds

☆ Describe the Result (£££/☺☺☺) – 30-60 seconds

Can you do it? Practise in advance. On page 106 there are some questions for you to practise with – and time yourself!

Pace and Passion

Vary the pace of your stories to add colour, which is more interesting than black and white. How can you tell a story in colour? Vary your:

• pitch – highs and lows

• volume – louder and softer

• speed – faster, slower, pause sometimes

• tone – stress certain important words

Remember Passion? Imagine you are all fired up after a day at work when something special (good or bad) happened and you are telling your friend all about it. You will automatically put colour and variety into your speech. You will pause, for effect, after a word you particularly want them to notice. You might even put in a question for suspense:

♡ Guess what?

♡ You'll never believe what she did......(pause).....(deep breath)....

♡ It was wonderful!

Watch them

While you are telling your story, watch your audience to see how they are reacting. If they show signs of losing concentration, be ready to change tack. How can you tell if you are boring them? It is usually obvious:

- you lose their eye contact
- they start looking at their notes
- they fidget
- they yawn
- they go to sleep? No, surely not...

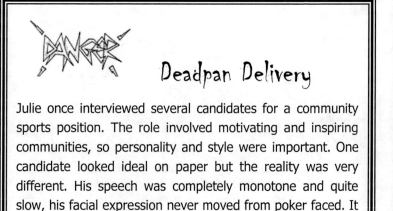

Deadpan Delivery

Julie once interviewed several candidates for a community sports position. The role involved motivating and inspiring communities, so personality and style were important. One candidate looked ideal on paper but the reality was very different. His speech was completely monotone and quite slow, his facial expression never moved from poker faced. It was really hard concentrating on what he was saying. The content was actually not bad, but she doubted his ability to keep communities awake, yet alone motivate them.

You don't have to be a bouncing ball of extraversion for all jobs, but it is worth thinking about how you come over, and how well it matches the demands of the role.

Wake them up

Use one of these techniques to bring them back:

- **speed up**: move quickly on to the STAR Result
- **pause**: look at them, take a breath, create suspense
- **ask a question**: "I wonder if you've heard of ...? Well, ..."
- **involve them**: "I don't know if this happens in your company ..."
- **check you are on the right track**: "Is this what you meant?" "Have I answered your question?"

All the time you are listening to the questions and telling your STAR stories, remember you are telling them in a way that shows:

1. You **can**
2. You *really* **want** this job in this company
3. You will **fit in**

So, your memo note to help you shine in the middle has five points:

1. **STAR**
2. **KISS**
3. **Pace & Passion**
4. **Watch them**
5. **Wake them up**

And always...
Be Confident

The End

You remember that people keep a fairly strong memory of the ending, so it is important to get it right. You want to end on a positive note.

You may still have some questions or be worried about things that could go wrong. Interviews can be run in many different ways, and the purpose of this book is to give you the tools to respond, whatever happens. The next section "What if...? and Frequently Asked Questions (FAQs) will look at many of your worries, including how to deal with the question that comes towards the end of most interviews: "Is there anything you would like to ask us?" Here we will take a quick look at the overall impression you are trying to give and how to make sure your response to this question does not spoil it.

Make sure your question reinforces that you want the job and you will fit in. Remember Respect? Whatever you choose to ask them at this last stage of the interview, It is best to avoid anything that suggests criticism or that you are interviewing them by putting them on the spot with a question they will find difficult to answer. You want their last memory of you to be a good one. See page 98-99 for some ideas.

The message you want them to receive boils down to just three points. This person...

- **can**
  - do this job and do it well
  - meet our needs
- **wants**
  - this job
  - to work in our organisation
- **will fit in**
  - with me as line manager
  - with the rest of the team
  - with our vision and culture
  - with our public image

Lastly, say good-bye and walk out as confidently as you came in. Be nice, and be the role. Your memo note to help you shine at the end has five points:

1. **Be the Role**
2. **Deep Breath**
3. **Eye Contact**
4. **Smile**
5. **Thank You**

And always...**Be Confident**

86

What if...?   Interview FAQs

Interviews can work in many different ways, depending on the organisation and the individuals conducting them. The **TAPAS** five step model will help you prepare by giving you the general principles behind any selection interview, which you can adapt to the situation you are faced with.

There are some situations that crop up so often that it is worth dealing with them here, so they do not take you by surprise or make you worry unduly beforehand. We will look at what to do if:

- It is a telephone interview
- You forget your STAR stories
- You do not meet all the criteria
- They ask about your weaknesses
- There is something in your work history you want to hide
- They ask a trick question
- They ask what salary you are looking for
- They describe a work problem and ask "What would you do?"
- It is a group interview or an assessment centre
- They ask if you have any questions for them

Telephone interviews

These are becoming more common as companies need to save money. Everything you have read here applies to telephone interviews, but with something missing – you cannot see your interviewer and they cannot see you. That sounds good. You do not have to worry about your clothes, your posture or your facial expression. Or do you? Because they cannot see you, you will have to do all the work with your voice. Call centre workers are trained to smile as they pick up the phone because the person at the other end can hear and feel the smile.

Here is a true story about John who had taken early retirement from his company. He still needed to work but, as he now had a small pension, he could take on a less stressful role. He knew that a company he used to work for wanted part-timers in a new branch. He had been well thought of there, and it was a job he was well qualified for and could easily do. He sent off an application form and was hopeful. A week or so later, he was just having his lunch when the phone rang. He did not recognise the number and thought it must be a sales call.

It was the new manager of the branch he had applied to, who thanked him for his application and immediately started asking him questions. John was shocked when, at the end of the conversation, she said they would not be taking his application further because he did not seem to show the enthusiasm or the quick thinking that they wanted.

It was not very fair to take him by surprise, but it could happen. It could also happen when you see the job advertised and phone for more details. Now you have been warned, you can be prepared. Have you checked the voicemail greeting on your phone?

Usually you will have warning of a telephone interview but even then, think about how you will show over the phone that you **can**, you **want to** and you will **fit in**. Remember too, that because they cannot see enthusiasm in your face, you may need to respond quickly to what they say, not leaving any silences. Even just "yes" or "I see" while you think of the answer is better than silence. And keep smiling!

What if I forget something – shall I take notes with me?

The danger of taking notes in is that you will try to read them rather than keep eye contact with the interviewers. An interview should be a conversation that flows naturally. If you look at notes, it suggests that you had to learn your lines and are acting a role rather than being yourself. Even in a telephone interview, we would not recommend trying to read from notes while you are talking.

What you can do is to have one small sheet of paper with a few words or bullet points on, that you can glance at while you sit outside the interview room and then quickly put away in your pocket or handbag before you go in. On that sheet, you can list in one or two words per bullet point, the employer's five or six key needs. Beside each one write key words to remind you of its STAR story. For example:

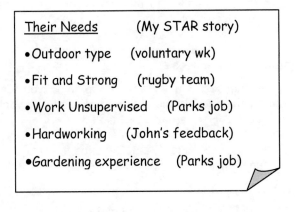

You could make one more memo to adjust your mindset for your entrance and their "Blink!" moment:

If you do not match all their criteria

Do not worry, this is not a problem for them – yet. They have read your application and they still called you for interview. Probably there was no one who could tick all their boxes so they are looking for the best fit. To show you have done your homework, you can tackle it head on by recognising your lack of experience in this area as a possible weakness and saying how you will overcome it. "A weakness for me in relation to this job is that I don't have any experience in .... However, I can ...." Read on.

Have you any weaknesses?

"I have no weaknesses" sounds rather arrogant but you do not want to tell them anything that could put them off, so what weaknesses should you reveal? Here are two techniques:

1. Every cloud has its silver lining. Describe a weakness that, in different circumstances, is actually a strength:

> Some people think I am fussy about detail.
>
> **But** this means everything I produce is perfect and you will never have complaints from customers.

> I love people and have been criticised for spending too long talking to them rather than completing my paperwork.
>
> **But** I think I can put my people skills to good use in this job which is all about team building and customer relations.

As part of your preparation toolkit, choose a weakness you have and note it here, showing how it can also be a strength...

> My weakness...
>
> **but...**

A warning – even if you tell them the silver lining to your weakness, they may still pick up on it and ask if it has ever caused problems for you. If so, be ready to answer this as you would the "mistake and lesson learned" question – see page 92-93.

2. Show that you have recognised a weakness and you know how to prevent it becoming a problem:

> I'm not really strong on detail, I'm much better at big picture and strategic thinking...
>
> **so** I always make sure someone else on the team checks the fine detail.

> I've not got a brilliant memory...
>
> **so** I always write everything down in my diary and task list. That way, nothing gets forgotten and I've got a record of everything.

Choose a weakness you have and describe it here, showing how you prevent it becoming a problem...

> My weakness...
>
> **so...**

Remember, if you know you do not match all their criteria, you can use that as your weakness and use your "**but**" to show them why this should not be a problem.

> I see you want someone with experience in construction as well as gardening. I haven't worked in the building trade...
>
> **But**... my dad taught me a lot and I've completely gutted the house we bought, installed new kitchen, bathroom, everything, so I think I can do most things.

Remember too, you have a choice. You do not have to tell them the worst thing about yourself. When you choose a weakness to reveal to them, go back to your analysis of the job in **TAPAS Step 2** and choose a weakness that could be a benefit rather than a problem for them. If the job requires keen attention to detail, you will choose the "fussy about detail" weakness rather than the "hate detail/prefer wider picture" one.

A question similar to the one about weaknesses is: "What is the worst mistake you have ever made?" Again, you do not have to tell them about your worst ever mistake - after all, it is a matter of opinion anyway. **It is your decision** which mistake to tell them about, so choose one that you learned from, telling them what you learned and how you avoided making the same mistake a second time. You can make it into a kind of STAR story:

A Mistake - and how I learned from it

★ Situation

In my first job I was an administrator and good at my work but very nervous talking to people. The manager had been asked to go and give a presentation about our service to a group of customers and I prepared his notes and slides.

★ Task

At the last minute, he was called away to a more important conference and he asked me to give the presentation in his place, as I knew the topic inside out.

Mistake

I froze with fear. I gave the presentation but I just read out the notes at top speed and then fled. I could tell people were bored and one of them even complained to my manager.

Lesson Learned

I realised my fear would prevent me progressing in my career and I had to get over it.

★ Actions

I saw an evening course in public speaking advertised at the local college and signed up. I really enjoyed learning the techniques they taught and eventually I began to actually enjoy giving talks.

★ Result

In my present job, marketing the service is an important part of my role, and I know my presentations always lead to increased business.

What mistake could you turn into a lesson learned?

A Mistake - and how I learned from it
⭐ **Situation**
⭐ **Task**
Mistake
Lesson Learned
⭐ **Actions**
⭐ **Result**

Try to choose a mistake where the lesson learned and the result are relevant to the job you are applying for. In the example, the person was applying for a job where networking and presentations were important. They also showed that by signing up for a course rather than waiting for the manager to send them on a course, they were self motivated and well organised.

Skeletons in the cupboard

There may be something in your work history that you do not want them to know. Maybe you were sacked from a job; had a long period of unemployment or travelling overseas; have had periods off work due to ill health. It could be that painful things happened to you: you were bullied at school; your boss picked on you; you did not pass certain exams.

If at all possible, it is best to keep the conversation on the bright side and avoid mentioning any past difficulties. This is because even if something was not your fault, your feelings about that event will start to affect your confidence and you will lose the positive attitude that you want to project.

However if you believe the employer will find out about the skeleton in the cupboard, you need to treat it like a weakness and work out a positive spin to put on it: "That happened a long time ago, I have learned from it and my recent work history has been excellent".

Some general rules to help you keep a positive spin are:

- When you describe past jobs, always find something good to say about them. If that is impossible, do not draw attention to them.
- Never criticise a past employer even if you think this interviewer will agree with you. They may not share your view and once you start being negative, it is hard to stop.
- Never lose your temper. Remember you are trying to empathise with the interviewers and see things from their point of view. Sometimes they may be testing your ability to keep calm under pressure. If you feel yourself getting irritated, show these skills: sit back in your chair, smile pleasantly, take a deep breath and then give a reasonable reply. If they get really offensive (very unlikely, but it has happened), you may decide that they are unprofessional and you would not want to work for them. Then the only way to keep your self-respect may be to get up and leave, firmly but keeping calm and polite so as not to descend to their level.

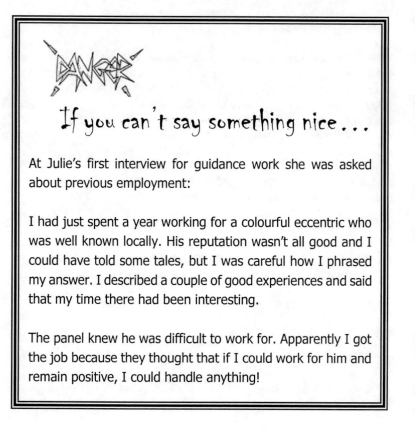

If you can't say something nice...

At Julie's first interview for guidance work she was asked about previous employment:

I had just spent a year working for a colourful eccentric who was well known locally. His reputation wasn't all good and I could have told some tales, but I was careful how I phrased my answer. I described a couple of good experiences and said that my time there had been interesting.

The panel knew he was difficult to work for. Apparently I got the job because they thought that if I could work for him and remain positive, I could handle anything!

Trick Questions

Employers are not usually trying to catch you out. They just want to get to know you so they can see how well you would meet their needs. They may want to take you by surprise though, partly because they know that people read books like this and are helped by advisers and coaches to prepare carefully. They may want to see what you do when you have no time to plan, just to get at "the real you". People report being asked questions like:

If you were an animal, what kind of animal would you be?

How should you react? Remember I **can** do the job, I **want** to do the job and I will **fit in**. To show you will fit in, you want to be a sport and join in the fun, so take it in good part and smile (rather than get irritated at such a pointless question). If possible, try to link your answer to their five or six key needs, using it to show you **can** do the job and that you are the right kind of person.

If you were aiming for the groundsperson job, you could say "I'd be a prize bull – I am strong and tough, I can take hard work and I like the outdoors, whatever the weather". For a leadership role you might say "I'd be a lion. I am a natural leader, I speak out for what is right and I can keep people focused even when things are difficult."

You do not have to link your answer so obviously to the job needs but whatever you say, join in the game. You could give an amusing answer but if you do, make sure you do not put yourself down. Without boasting, still aim to describe yourself in a good light.

What salary are you looking for?

In the public sector the salary is usually set but in the commercial sector it can often be negotiable. Some people are used to negotiating and enjoy it but if you are not, it is best to think this one through in advance so you are not thrown by the question.

You do not want to price yourself out of the market but nor do you want to undervalue your worth and of course you want to earn as much as possible. You could state a figure or you could tell them what you are earning now and indicate you would only move for a rise of at least so many thousand. If you are taking on extra responsibilities, you can state how much you think those are worth.

Before deciding on the figures, it is a good idea to do some research into what is the rate for the job and how this firm usually pays compared to the average. This will help you sound more objective. "I understand that pay for this kind of job is usually in the £... to £... band" will be more convincing than just saying "I want £..." If relevant, you might add that with your experience, you would hope to be paid closer to the upper end of the scale.

Remember that if they ask what salary you are hoping for, they expect you to negotiate. Do not worry too much about asking too high a figure. They are likely to respond with another lower figure and continue to negotiate until you come to an agreement.

Scenarios: What would you do?

One quite common interview question is to present you with a scenario that could happen in the role you are applying for and ask you how you would handle it. As they listen to your answer, they will be judging both your knowledge and your general approach. To help them really believe how you would act, it would be good to link the scenario to something similar that you have already handled and make that into a STAR story. Start by telling them how you would handle it, bringing in as much of relevant background knowledge as you can, and then say "something similar happened when..."

Group Interviews

You may arrive at the interview to find yourself in a room full of people sitting in a circle or round a table. This could be the main part of the interview or you could have been invited to an assessment centre where a group discussion is just one of the exercises they will use to assess you.

The main reason for telling you this is so that you will not be taken by surprise. Why do they hold group interviews? Maybe they want to see:

- how you get on with others – can you give and take?
- whether you can speak out and be heard
- how you can argue your point and win people round
- what type of role you take on in a group: team player? leader? ideas person?

You will probably want to strike a balance so that you contribute and say something, without shouting everyone else down. Show you can listen, think before you speak, but try to take a turn at speaking. Remember, they may be watching and assessing the whole time you are on the premises. Be the person you want to be – the role you are aiming for.

Assessment Centres

This term is used to describe a method of selection. If you are invited to an assessment centre, this will be an event where more than one selection activity takes place. There will almost certainly be a face to face interview, but there also may be: pencil and paper tests; online questionnaires; role plays; group or team activities; a presentation (you will probably be given the title to prepare in advance although sometimes they will ask you to think on your feet); a case study to discuss or write about. Find out as much as you can in advance, so you can prepare. The Human Resources people will usually be happy to tell you the programme they have planned.

Have you any questions for us?

You will not feel very clever if you have to answer: "No". It is wise to have one or two questions prepared and there are some pitfalls to avoid.

Interviewers only have a short time slot for you to ask your questions, usually towards the end of the interview. One question is probably quite sufficient and preferably one that they can answer quite easily and quickly. While you want to show your in-depth knowledge of the company or its business, questions that require a complex answer or touch on commercially sensitive information will put the interviewers on the spot, which will not give them a good feeling about you.

It is best not to ask about things that imply you only care about the money and the holidays. Either find out about pay, hours and conditions before attending the interview, or wait until you are offered the job (by this time they have decided they want you so you are in a stronger position).

Good questions show:

- **you are keen enough to have found out about the company**:

"I see you have several branches across the Midlands. Might I be sent to work in other towns?"

Note that if you ask this question, they may come back with "would that be a problem for you?" so decide in advance how you feel about that and how to answer it.

- **you have found out about the company and you have some additional skills you want to make them aware of:**

"I understand you are expanding into overseas markets. Would there be much travel in this role and would my fluent French, Spanish and Chinese be useful to you?"

- **your enthusiasm for the work or your commitment to the company:**

"Would I be able to work in every aspect of your business?"

"Would I be trained in new applications and take on other duties as I progressed?"

"Would I be able to continue with my study towards the AAT qualification?"

"What are the opportunities for promotion?"

- **If your prepared questions have been answered, do not worry. You can turn your question into one last bid for the job, for example:**

"Is there anything more you need to know about me?"

"I'd just like to say that now I've met you I'm very interested in this job, and I hope I have shown I have everything you are looking for."

"As I understand it, you are looking for someone who .... and I believe I have shown how my experience, abilities and interests match up. Is there anything else you would like to know about me?"

- **Or you can simply say:**

"I was going to ask about .... but you have answered all the questions I had, thank you."

Why not prepare one or two questions now and at the same time note down anything else you need to research about the company to help you ask intelligent questions.

Questions to ask them

Research needed

What if...? Last minute practicalities

What if... I get lost

Preparation is the key. Ideally you will do a dry run a week or so beforehand, making sure you know what the traffic will be doing at that time of day or checking the train or bus times. Time the journey and work out what time you will need to leave home. Get a map or street plan if you think you will forget. In case you still get lost on the day, have enough money with you to jump in a taxi and let them find the way. Have your mobile charged and put their number in your contacts list so you can ring for directions if you cannot find them any other way.

What if... I'm late

Try to avoid being late by foreseeing what could make you late. Check on the internet before you leave for any traffic problems or cancelled trains. Give yourself some leeway by arriving earlier than you need to and work out where you can wait if you are too early. Again, have their number handy on your mobile so you can phone them quickly in an emergency and let them know. If you keep them informed, they will be sympathetic.

What if... I arrive too early

How early is too early? You will try not to arrive more than ten minutes before your interview time, but it is not always possible to fine tune your journey. If you drove there, you have the advantage of waiting in your car if you have time to kill. If you intend to go by bus or train, then on your trial run you can look for somewhere comfortable to sit and wait, either nearby or in the building itself where there may be a large general reception area. If the weather is fine you may prefer to walk round the block – exercise is good for keeping nerves at bay. If it is raining or not the kind of area that is pleasant to walk around, go into the building, explain to the receptionist that you are early for your interview and ask if there is somewhere you can wait.

What if... The weather's bad and I get soaked or hot and sweaty
Your preparation should have included checking the weather forecast and wearing suitable clothing and footwear. If weather conditions are extreme, it may be worth paying out for a taxi to get you there dry or cool. If you have had to bring coat, scarf, gloves, now wet umbrella, you will not want to clutter yourself up with these in the interview. Speak nicely to the receptionist or secretary and ask if there is somewhere you can leave them.

If you are hot and bothered, freshen up by using some lightly perfumed wipes (avoid strong perfume just before going into the room, as people may find it overpowering). Anxiety can make you dehydrated, so have a good drink of water (remember tea and coffee are dehydrating too). Water will freshen your breath, but you could suck a mint as well. Have a tissue or a freshly laundered handkerchief to hold in your hand and absorb moisture, especially just before the beginning and end of the interview when you may have to shake hands.

What if... I don't know whether to shake hands
This is a difficult one. Some people and cultures expect it, others do not. Follow the "Let Them Lead" rule here and you will not go wrong. This means having your right hand ready to shake, then observing them to see whether they put their hand forward to shake with you.

What if... I have to wait in a room with all the other candidates
On the plus side, they are people to talk to. Chatting can calm your nerves and warm you up ready to shine in the interview. On the minus side, your confidence could ebb away if you think they look and sound "better" than you. If you get too involved in talking with them, you may use up your energy before your interview. There again, you might learn some useful information on the size of the competition and you might be one of those people who are fired up to work harder to sell yourself now you know what you have to beat.

On balance, some general chit-chat will make you seem friendly and help you relax, but it is OK to politely cut it short when you have had enough. Have something with you to read (your last minute memos and confidence boosters, the job description). You can also check your mobile and make sure it is now turned off. Do not be tempted to text friends while you are waiting. How professional will it look if you miss the call to interview because you are glued to your mobile?

What if... They keep me waiting ages

You would expect someone to keep you informed and if not, hopefully there will be someone there – receptionist, secretary, human resources staff – that you can ask what time you can expect to be called in. If you are worried about your train home, you can discuss this with them.

Where is the Starting Line?

Kathryn made a good impression on the interview panel. She was highly professional in her approach and well prepared for the interview. She scored very highly in her answers and appeared friendly and enthusiastic.

Did she get the job? Not a chance! What Kathryn didn't realise was that companies often seek the views of reception staff when recruiting, to give them another perspective on the candidates. Due to being anxious, she had been rude and dismissive to the receptionist on her arrival.

The interview starts the minute your foot steps over the threshold. Anyone you come into contact with may be asked about you, so be prepared.

What if... They talk about my application form or CV and I've forgotten what I wrote

Now you have read this, this will not happen because you will make sure you keep a copy, bring it with you and read it on your journey or while you wait. Do put it away before you go into the interview room, though. If you try to glance at it during the interview you will end up fumbling, losing concentration and breaking eye contact. Trust yourself – you will remember.

What if... My mind goes blank and I dry up

Try not to panic. This can happen to anyone and the interviewers will understand the effect of nerves. It is fine to come clean and admit it. Take a deep breath, look at the interviewers, smile and say "I'm sorry, I've lost my thread. Would you mind repeating the question?" When they ask their question again, it will help you to focus if you repeat some of the key words aloud. For example, they ask: "How would you deal with a team member who had lost motivation?" and you repeat: "A team member who is de-motivated..." This makes you seem thoughtful and to be taking their question seriously. It will fix it in your mind and give you time to think of an incident to turn into a STAR story.

What if... Something goes wrong that I haven't thought of yet

You cannot expect to prepare for everything in advance. Accept that you will do your best to get it right, but it is OK to make mistakes. Some of us have gone to interviews, made every mistake in the book, and then been offered the job! Others have done everything perfectly and been turned down. Come clean, apologise and offer to try again. Most interviewers will find your honesty refreshing. You will have done your best and you will have learned a huge amount that will stand you in good stead in the future. Good for you!

Confidence

On your way to the interview, or shortly before you go in, here are some positive thoughts to read through and say to yourself...

- I am a worthwhile person and I deserve respect.

- I know what I am good at, and I can prove it.

- I know what I like doing, and I can talk about it.

- I know what I like about this employer / company.

- I'm going to like the interviewers and I'll help them find out all the good things about me.

- I shall choose what to tell the interviewers and what not to tell them.

- I know my strengths and weaknesses. My weaknesses can also be strengths, and I know how to deal with them.

- I am proud of my achievements.

- I feel enthusiastic.

- I feel confident.

- I can do this job.

- I want this job.

- I feel good.

Practice Interview Questions

Following **TAPAS Step 3**, having analysed the job to identify the employer's key needs and then written STAR stories to use as evidence of how you can meet them, it is a good idea to prepare to tell these stories in the interview. It is one thing to have them in your head and to write notes on paper, and quite another thing to decide on the spot which to use in answer to a question and to tell it convincingly.

So find a supportive friend and ask them to role play an interview with you. Tell them the job you are going for, give them your list of the five or six key needs and let them read the job description if there is one. Then set up an interview room, go outside and when you are both ready, you can knock and walk in.

Here is a script for your friend to use (questions not in bold are optional)

1. **Good Afternoon, ... (your name), I am ...., the Section Manager / Director, and this is Karen Jones, our HR Manager. Please come in and take a seat.**

2. **I hope you had a good journey. Did you find us easily?**

3. *As you know, we are looking for a .... (the position) and we were impressed with your application so we wanted to get to know you a bit better. I will be conducting most of the interview and Karen is here to observe and answer any of your questions that I am unsure of.

4. **Can you tell us what attracted you to this position?**

5. *Please tell us a little about your career so far, and what you have most enjoyed.

Look at the list of 5 or 6 key needs and for one or more of these ask:
6. **We need someone who can .... Can you give me an example of when you have handled this kind of task successfully?**

7. *Please give an example of when you have overcome a communication problem with a colleague or customer

8. **Please give an example of a weakness or a mistake you have made and how you have dealt with it or what you learned.**

9. *Do you have any worries or foresee any challenges for you in this role?

10. *Where do you see yourself in five years' time?

11. **Well, thank you for everything you have told us so far. Is there anything you would like to add, or do you have any questions for us?**

12. **Right, if you have no more questions, we will now end the interview, and thank you very much for coming in today.**

*If you are short of time, leave out these questions and just ask the questions in **bold**.

How did you do?

After your role play interview, ask your friend to sit down with you and review it. Depending on how much time you have, here are two sets of questions. First, the short version, which you can also use on your own to review yourself, or following a real interview:

	✓	?	??
Entrance	✓	?	??
Looked the part?			
Looked friendly?			
Eye contact and smiling?			
Calm movements, sat down easily?			
First Words	✓	?	??
Confident?			
Showed was listening?			
Took lead from interviewer?			
Responded suitably?			
The Discussion	✓	?	??
Gave evidence of **ability** for <u>this</u> job?			
☆Described **Situation**			
☆Described **Task**			
☆Described **Actions**			
☆Described **Results**			
Showed **enthusiasm** for this job?			
Listened and responded well?			
Did not say too little?			
Did not ramble on too long?			
Handled awkward questions?			
The Close	✓	?	??
Ended on a positive note?			
Walked out confidently?			

Here is the long version, if you have time and want to review every question and answer in detail. Ask your friend to comment on each.

1. **Good Afternoon, ...** (your name), **I am ...., the Section Manager / Director, and this is Karen Jones, our HR Manager. Please come in and take a seat.**

What impression did you get of the candidate as they walked in and took their seat? Did they...
- ☐ *look the part?*
- ☐ *look friendly?*
- ☐ *look confident?*
- ☐ *keep eye contact?*
- ☐ *smile?*
- ☐ *look enthusiastic?*
- ☐ *seem relaxed?*

2. **I hope you had a good journey. Did you find us easily?**

Did they...
- ☐ *give a positive answer?*
- ☐ *say a bit more than just yes, but not too much detail?*
- ☐ *sound at ease and competent?*

3. **Good. Well, as you know, we are looking for a .... (the position) and we were impressed with your application so we wanted to get to know you a bit better. I will be conducting most of the interview and Karen is here to observe and answer any of your questions that I am unsure of.**

- ☐ *Were they listening attentively as you told them this?*
- ☐ *What made you feel listened to (or not)?*

4. **Can you tell us what attracted you to this position?**

Did they...

☐ *list some of the main features of the job (as per their list of five or six key needs)?*
☐ *state why it appeals to them?*
☐ *say why they believe they will be good in the role?*

5. Please tell us a little about your career so far, and what you have most enjoyed.

Did you get...
☐ *a clear picture of the path they have followed up to now?*
☐ *some idea that they have the skills for this job?*

6. We need someone who can .... Can you give me an example of when you have handled this kind of task successfully?

Did they tell a story that was...
☐ *relevant?*
☐ *interesting?*
☐ *in enough detail but not too long?*
☐ *describe what they personally did?*
☐ *say how that led to a good outcome?*

7. Please give an example of when you have overcome a communication problem with a colleague or customer

Did they tell a story that was...
☐ *relevant to the **role** and the **level** of job they are applying for?*
☐ *interesting?*
☐ *in enough detail but not too long?*
☐ *describe what they personally did and what was the outcome?*

8. Please give an example of a weakness or a mistake you have made and how you have dealt with it or learned from it

☐ *Did they give an example that was relevant?*
☐ *After hearing the story, do you believe that this weakness will be a problem in this job role?*

9. **Do you have any worries or foresee any challenges for you in this role?**

☐ *Did they show realistic knowledge of the job and the organisation?*
☐ *Did they convince you that they would overcome the challenge and make it work?*

10. **Where do you see yourself in five years' time?**

Did they show...
☐ *ambition and commitment to work hard?*
☐ *enthusiasm for your company and/or for their chosen career?*
☐ *knowledge and understanding of the company and the job?*
☐ *a desire to push you out of your job and take over?*

11. **Thank you for everything you have told us so far. Is there anything you would like to add, or do you have any questions for us?**

☐ *Did their questions or comments show they want the job?*
☐ *Did they tell you any more to show they were right for the job?*
☐ *Did they ask too many questions?*

12. **Right, if you have no more questions, we will now end the interview, and thank you very much for coming in today.**

☐ *Did they say Thank You and Good-Bye in a confident and pleasant manner?*
☐ *Could you now visualise them in the job role?*

Any further comments or advice to this person?

If you cannot find a friend to role play, you can record yourself. You could speak out the questions first and then answer them. When you have finished, play it back and use the feedback sheets to assess yourself.

Next time

You have told the interviewers that you learn from your mistakes. You can also learn from what you did well. Now you know what to keep doing and what to change, you can make an action plan.

Action Plan

To help me prepare for the next interview, I will:

At the interview, I will try to:

Signed:.....................................

Date:......................................

Final Checklist – The week before

Gather papers and make sure they fit in the bag you will be taking:

- ☐ Job ad or job description for this job
- ☐ Other paperwork you have received from the employer
- ☐ Check you have their phone number, name of admin person
- ☐ Your job analysis (**TAPAS Step 2**)
- ☐ Your employer research (**TAPAS Step 2**)
- ☐ Your list of six STAR story titles (**TAPAS Step 2**)
- ☐ Your six STAR stories (**TAPAS Step 2**)
- ☐ Your confidence boosters (**TAPAS Steps 4 and 5**)
- ☐ You memo lists (**TAPAS Step 5**)

- ☐ Put up your Self Talk sticky labels and read each one out loud morning and evening (**TAPAS Step 4**)

Research online or by asking people:

- ☐ Location and maps
- ☐ Train or bus times if needed
- ☐ Usual salaries for this type of work

- ☐ Do a dry run of the journey, time it and look for where you could wait if you arrive early. Maybe check out how safe the area is, too, if you will have to wait outside the building.

- ☐ Book and buy bus or rail tickets if needed

- ☐ Get your hair trimmed (maybe also coloured, styled)
- ☐ Choose your outfit, try it on and get it clean and ready

- ☐ Do a practise interview with a friend, get feedback and write your action plan

Final Checklist – The day before

☐ Read through all the paperwork you gathered during the week
☐ Check your interview practice action plan
☐ Put your memo lists, job analysis and six STAR story titles in your pocket or handbag – even more easy to get at than the other paperwork you will be taking
☐ Check the weather forecast and adjust your wardrobe accordingly
☐ Check train or traffic updates
☐ Put the employer's contact details in your mobile
☐ Put a bottle of water and some mints in your bag
☐ Put in your bag a small packet of wipes, tissues, a handkerchief
☐ Check you have enough cash to get a taxi if you need to

Final Checklist – in the evening

☐ Eat a light, easily digestible meal – no rich food, try to avoid alcohol or too much caffeine (keep the treats and rewards for tomorrow evening)
☐ Put all your clothes out ready – leave nothing to chance
☐ Charge your mobile
☐ Check your travel times and put them in your bag
☐ Set your alarm
☐ Early night - Sleep well!

Read more about it

We wanted to keep this book short so that you could focus on the five steps of **TAPAS** that we believe will prepare you well for your interview on the day. The jobs featured as examples in this book were fairly basic and straightforward so perhaps you want to know more about interviews for your kind of work or your professional level. You may now want more detail on how to get invited to interview in the first place with application forms and CVs, or about topics we have touched on like body language, communication, image, dress, difficult questions, assessment centres, psychometric tests.

For this reason we have selected some books that can be bought from a bookseller or borrowed from your local library. Remember you can always ask your library to buy a book for you if they do not already stock it and second-hand books can often be bought cheaply online. We have not mentioned every book on job interviews and there is not even space to list all those we like. Here are just a few titles on the different topics you may want to research further. A few DVDs we have found useful are included too, as well as some agencies you can go to for advice.

The whole job hunting process

You're Hired – CVs, Interview Answers and Psychometric Tests – 3 career books in one. 2011, by Corinne Mills, Ceri Roderick, James Meachin and Stephan Lucks, published by Trotman.

A book aimed at managerial and executive interviewees, written by blue chip company recruiters and a career management coach. The CV section offers templates for different types of CV (chronological, functional, one-page and your own CV website).

The interview section explains competency interviews and suggests how to prepare, with tips on first impressions and the effects of different behaviours. There are examples of questions you may be asked, divided into categories, each one with a "poor answer", a "better answer" and an explanation. The psychometric section explains the different types of assessment with examples to try, and the answers.

CV and Interview Handbook. 2008, by Sue Tumelty, published by Which? Guides.

A briefer look at the whole process from deciding what you want from a job and where to look for vacancies, through writing CVs, dealing with recruitment agencies and headhunters, online applications, to interviews and negotiating the deal. It points out that in summer 2007, a poll by the Association of Graduate Recruiters found 76.9% of their employers would only accept applications made online. There is a section on using online methods at all stages of the process, including social and professional networking sites.

How to get a job in a recession. 2009, by Denise Taylor, published by Brook House Press.

There is an introduction about the changing job market, coping with redundancy and practical ideas for organising your time and planning your job search. The CV section has detailed advice on the component parts, words to use, layout and examples of three types of CV – chronological, skills-based and combination. Different ways to find opportunities include networking and the hidden job market. As well as chapters on interview preparation and the interview itself, there is advice on handling phone interviews, psychometric tests and assessment centres and finally on salary negotiation.

Interview Questions and Answers

Job Interviews – Top answers to tough questions. 2008 (revised edition), by John Lees and Matthew J Deluca, published by McGraw Hill Professional.

This book lists 201 questions you may be asked and suggests how to answer them. The format makes it easy to use. All the questions are listed at the front, divided into topics or stages of the interview. A few of these are clearly asterisked as being the most important – very helpful if you are short of time.

There are some chapters explaining how interviews work, where to look for jobs and how to get shortlisted. Each of the remaining eleven chapters focuses on a group of questions you may be asked at each stage of the interview, suggesting how to respond and what you are aiming to do by answering in that way. There is a chapter on difficult questions which includes how to deal with illegal or unethical ones.

Tough Interview Questions and How to Answer Them. 2009, by Rachel Adamson and Mandy Soule, published by Which? Guides.

Clear and concise presentation make this book easy to read. For each question there are a few bullet points and one line suggestions, together with a short example answer. It gives some ideas of what to ask when they say "have you any questions for us?", and how to respond to illegal questions that they should not have asked. There is also a chapter on assessment centres.

Great Answers to Tough Interview Questions. 2011 (8th edition), by Martin John Yate, published by Kogan Page.

Now in its 8th edition, this was probably the first book to list questions and suggest how to answer them. There are sections covering finding vacancies, making contact, telephone interviews, what to wear and body language. 100 pages of questions are broadly organised into topics: background, experience and competence; personality; stress interviews; school and college leavers. At the end there is advice on negotiating the offer and turning defeat into victory.

Ultimate Interview – Make a great impression and get that job. 2008 (2nd edition), by Lynn Williams, published by Kogan Page.

The unique selling point of this book is that its questions and answers are tailored to different jobs, so you do not waste time reading questions you are unlikely to be asked. The jobs covered are: practical jobs; creative jobs; clerical and administrative jobs; sales and marketing; technical; management; customer relations; questions for school and college leavers. There are some general questions anyone could be asked, especially difficult questions and tricky questions.

Confidence, Body Language and Personal Presentation

You're Hired! Tips and techniques for a brilliant interview. 2009, by Judi James, published by Trotman.

Judi James is an expert in the field of body language and behaviour, and focuses on these aspects of the interview. She gives tips in a lively style on adjusting your mindset: "Learning to love interviews", "How to re-boot your confidence" and on adjusting your image: "Dress the part" and "Talk the talk". There is advice on giving presentations, and how to behave in group interviews, as well as a chapter that tackles anxieties such as struggling with eye contact.

The Interview Expert – How to get the job you want. 2012, by John Lees, published by Pearson Education Ltd.

This new book by John Lees focuses on what is really going on in an interview and how you can influence it – as we have in this book but in more depth. His experience as a career coach shines through as he explores why interviews go wrong and gives insights into handling interview nerves, how to tell your stories, different strategies needed for introverts and extraverts, how to get good feedback and how to learn from it. He has asked employers what impresses them and what puts them off, both in a CV and in interviews, and shares this with us. In all, a very interesting book, especially if you are looking for a fresh approach and a deeper understanding.

Blink! The Power of Thinking without Thinking. 2006, by Malcolm Gladwell, published by Penguin Books.

This book proposes that intuitive, snap judgements can be as effective as those that are carefully and rationally thought through and gives many examples to illustrate the point.

Silent Messages: Implicit communication of emotions and attitudes. 1981 (2nd edition), by Albert Mehrabian, published by Wadsworth, California.

Albert Mehrabian is an academic, currently a professor of Psychology in California, and was one of the first people to highlight the power of non verbal communication.

Psychometrics and Assessment Centres

How to Succeed at an Assessment Centre. 2011 (3rd edition) by Harry Tolley and Robert Wood, published by Kogan Page.

The authors are a professor and a psychologist who specialise in assessment and selection and have run assessment centres for large employers. This book gives a thorough explanation on all aspects of how assessment centres are run, explained clearly and concisely, with plenty of examples. There are chapters on: Group exercises; Presentations; Psychometric tests; Personality, Motivation and Emotional Intelligence questionnaires; Panel interviews; In-tray and Case Study exercises; Role plays. There are some questionnaires for self-assessment in all the competences expected of high flyers, to help you plan to develop so you can be successful in all areas.

Brilliant Psychometric and Other Tests

This book is one of the *Brilliant* series, which also includes *Brilliant... CV, Interviews, Answers to Tough Interview Questions, Career Finder, Job Hunter*

How to Pass...

A series published by Kogan Page. Titles include *How to Pass... Graduate Psychometric Tests, Professional Level Psychometric Tests, Verbal Reasoning Tests, Advanced Numeracy Tests, Data Interpretation Tests, QTS Numeracy and Literacy Skills.*

Presentations

Knockout Job Interview Presentations: How to Present with Confidence, Beat the Competition and Impress Your Way into a Top Job. 2010, by Rebecca Corfield, published by Kogan Page.

This book helps you to understand what employers are looking for and how to provide it through your presentation. It takes you through the whole process of planning so that you know what to include and how to present it. There are tips on coping with both seen and unseen briefs, making the practical preparations, then getting it right on the day, handling nerves and making an impact. It also looks into things that could go wrong, giving advice on how to rise above them and continue with your presentation unscathed.

DVDs

It is all very well to read about it, but with something so physical as an interview, how helpful it would be to watch one and see how it should be done. Seeing the effects of doing it badly can also be very instructive. Online videos come and go, for example there are many on YouTube.

Jumpcut Ltd (www.jumpcutuk.com) produce educational videos/DVDs, complete with training notes, which you may find at your local careers centre, school or college:

DVDs aimed at a wide age range, including those with experience:

Against All Odds. Three people attend an interview for the same job – compare their performance and work out who did best. Shows how to support your statements with evidence.

Interviewers from Hell. How to make the best of an interview by an untrained interviewer, ones who ramble, are disorganised, forgetful, aggressive or just not interested. Shows how to take control and turn the situation to your own advantage.

DVDs aimed at younger people include:

First Impressions – A Second Look *(2010)*. How to prepare, research, plan, dress and behave.

Say it again, Sam. How to change a poor performance into a good one.

The Interview Doctor. What employers want in an employee – attitudes and interview behaviours.

One to one advice

Career Coaching, Interview Practice

You may have access to free career guidance and coaching, especially if you are studying at school, college or university. There are government funded careers advisory services for adults in the UK – find your local centre via their websites:

England – www.nextstep.direct.gov.uk

Wales – www.careerswales.com

Scotland – www.skillsdevelopmentscotland.co.uk (click Tools)

Northern Ireland – www.nidirect.gov.uk/careers

Note that services offered via government funding are going through some change, so we are only able to reflect the situation at the time of publication. If in doubt, your local Jobcentre or library should signpost you to the right place.

It can be a good investment to pay for advice from a qualified professional career coach or guidance practitioner. Look on the website of:

Institute of Career Guidance – www.icg-uk.org

Image Consultants

Television makeover shows are always popular and it is amazing to see how people like us can be transformed through careful choice of clothing and hairstyle. If you decide to use an image consultant you should find their approach is personal and supportive, listening to who you really are and taking your taste and budget into account.

They work on the basis that your personal presentation contributes strongly to your impact and influence in the workplace. Overall, their message is: "Dress for the job you want, not for the job you've got."

You can choose what to work on with your consultant, but you are likely to cover:
- Colour: the shades that work for you
- Style, scale, proportion: making the most of your shape and size
- Grooming, make-up and accessories
- Planning a wardrobe, and effective shopping to make the most of your budget

Look for a consultant near you, phone a few and choose the one who appeals most to you (ask their prices too). Find members of:

First Impressions   www.firstimpressions.uk.com

Index